D0773164

THE GIFT
OF YEARS

THE GIFT OF YEARS

Growing Older Gracefully

JOAN CHITTISTER

NOVALIS

This book is dedicated to
Eunice Kennedy
whose life
—lived to the fullest at every stage—
has given life to many,
is model to us all.

Jacket design by Angel Guerra

Cover art by The Bridgeman Art Library (Stanhope Alexander Forbes [1857–1947], *Mrs Forbes, the artist's mother*)

Text design by Cynthia Dunne

Published by
B l u e B r i d g e
An imprint of
United Tribes Media Inc.
240 West 35th Street, Suite 500
New York, NY 10001

www.bluebridgebooks.com

Published in Canada by Novalis, Saint Paul University, Ottawa
Business Offices:

Novalis Publishing Inc.
10 Lower Spadina Avenue, Suite 400
Toronto, Ontario M5V 2Z2

Novalis Publishing Inc.
4475 Frontenac Street
Montréal, Québec H2H 2S2

Phone: 1-800-387-7164
Fax: 1-800-204-4140
E-mail: books@novalis.ca
www.novalis.ca

Library and Archives Canada Cataloguing in Publication: C2008-900759-X

ISBN: 978-2-89507-942-2

Novalis acknowledges the financial support of the Government of Canada through the Book Publishing Industry Development Program (BPIDP) for its publishing activities.

CONTENTS

INTRODUCTION: *The Purpose of Life*   vii

REGRET   1

MEANING   7

FEAR   13

AGEISM   21

JOY   27

AUTHORITY   33

TRANSFORMATION   39

NEWNESS   45

ACCOMPLISHMENT   51

POSSIBILITY   55

ADJUSTMENT   59

FULFILLMENT   67

MYSTERY   73

RELATIONSHIPS   79

TALE-TELLING   85

LETTING GO   89

LEARNING   95

RELIGION   101

FREEDOM   107

SUCCESS   113

TIME   117

WISDOM   123

SADNESS   129

DREAMS   133

LIMITATIONS   137

SOLITUDE   143

PRODUCTIVITY   149

MEMORIES   153

FUTURE   159

AGELESSNESS   163

IMMEDIACY   167

NOSTALGIA   173

SPIRITUALITY   179

LONELINESS   185

FORGIVENESS   189

OUTREACH   195

THE PRESENT   201

APPRECIATION   207

FAITH   211

LEGACY   215

AFTERWORD: *The Twilight Time*   219

Endnotes

Acknowledgments

INTRODUCTION
The Purpose of Life

It is a January morning in County Kerry. The Atlantic Ocean, off the coast of the craggy islands below me, is roiled with whitecaps and angry palisades of water crashing against the tiny islets in their rocky midst. The windstorms of the last two nights have drenched the hills on which this small Irish stone cottage clings, left them dripping water from bare branches hours later, sent the tiny rivulet of water outside my window rushing wildly down the mountainside to the valley below. It is an average Kerry winter day.

But not average for some. In the last two days of rocking, howling wind, five Irish fishermen and their trawler have been reported missing at sea. This morning, they were pronounced dead, the sea too wild yet to even attempt to recover their bodies.

Who they were, how old they were, I do not know. But one thing I do know: life and time are ghosted creatures for us all. They belong to us—and are not ours at the same time. Some of us, like these fishermen caught in a season's windstorm, leave it by surprise. Most of us, like you and me, inch our way through life, sure on the one hand that it will never end, certain on the other that it will surely be ending for us soon.

It is at moments of such quiet consciousness that it is important to come face-to-face with what it means to age, to be older, to be old, to become an elder in society. It is important that age be no impediment to the magnet for life in us. But life is not about breathing only. Life is about becoming more than we are, about being all that we can be. Whatever we are doing, however old we are, wherever we fall on the social-economic scale.

This is a book for those who are on the brink of "old age," for those who have just received their first mail message from the Association of Retired People, and knowing themselves to be young and healthy, are very surprised by it.

But this book is as much for those who are concerned about their parents and the kinds of issues older age may be raising in them. It is also for those who want to reflect on the gradual effects of the aging process in their own lives.

This is, finally, a book for those who do not "feel" old, whatever their chronological age, but who one day realize with a kind of numbing astonishment that they have not managed to elude it. They are older than they ever thought they could possibly become. They are now called "seniors" or "the elders" or "the older generation," even "elderly," by the young ones around them, despite the fact that inside themselves they feel no different now than they did a year ago. Except for the telling of the years, of course. And, in the end, those make all the difference.

Indeed, they are old and getting older by the day. At least as far as calendar days go. But inside, they know themselves to be coming out of one part of life and going into another, clinging to one but unable to stop themselves from slipping into the other. And they don't know what to think about it. Is this the end of everything they know to be good and fulfilling in life? Should they simply defer to the inevitable and accept their weary state? Or is it only the beginning of a whole new kind of life? Are they at the moment of purposelessness? Or is the purpose of life only now becoming visible? Since many of us might spend nearly as many years out of the work force as in it, it is surely necessary, surely right, to give thought to what these years hold, what they demand, what they have to offer us all. But that depends on whether or not we know what to look for as they come.

The thing most wrong about this book could well be that I may be too young to write it. I am, after all, only seventy. So, in the interest of full disclosure, I reserve the right to revise this edition when I am ninety.

For now, however, I will write about what it feels like to be facing that time of life for which there is no career plan.

I will write about what I have seen in the older people I have lived with all my life, who go about living vital years past the time most people would call their "productive" ones.

I will write about the transition into this last period of human growth and the way it can be lived as a summit-time of life.

There are, gerontologists tell us, three stages of "old" in our society. There are the young old, sixty-five to seventy-four years old; the old old, seventy-five to eighty-four; and the oldest old, at eighty-five years and over. All of these stages have some things in common—and each of them faces specific issues at the same time.

Unlike early life—life from birth to the age of twenty-one—relatively little has ever really been known about older age. In fact, gerontology as a science—the study of the biological, psychological, and social aspects of aging—didn't even begin until after World War II. Up until that time, any interest in age concentrated entirely on the means of prolonging youth or reversing the effects of aging. What gerontology is still lacking, however, is the awareness of the spiritual dimensions of the only part of life that gives us the resources we need to make a long-term evaluation of the nature and meaning of life itself.

I will write about life beyond its physical dimension, to its spiritual development. In fact, as the physical dimension of life diminishes, the spiritual dimension commonly increases. But I will not be writing about the physical changes that come with age—as important and impacting as these are. I will be writing instead about the mental and spiritual attitudes we bring to these challenges that really determine who we become as we advance from one stage of growing older to the next.

I will not be writing about death itself. Death and age are not synonyms. Death can come at any time. Age comes only to the truly blessed. I will write, of course, on what it means to know, consciously and clearly, that we ourselves are drawing closer to that time.

I will write about you and me and the significance of this time for all the years behind us as well as all the days ahead. And there will be many.

The gift of years comes to many more than realize that these later years *are* gift, not burden. Not everyone who lives them either understands them or welcomes them. This book is about the enterprise of embracing the blessings of this time and overcoming the burdens of it. That is the spiritual task of later life.

This is a special period of life—maybe the most special of them all. But with it come all the fears and hopes of a lifetime. To live these years well, we need to look at every one of the fears and hopes head up and alive. Life is not about age, about the length of years we manage to eke out of it. It is about aging, about living into the values offered in every stage of life. As E. M. Forster wrote, "We must be willing to let go of the life we have planned, so as to have the life that is waiting for us."

It is time for us to let go of both our fantasies of eternal youth and our fears of getting older, and to find the beauty of what it means to age well. It is time to understand that the last phase of life is not non-life; it is a *new* stage of life. These older years—reasonably active, mentally alert, experienced and curious, socially important and spiritually significant—are meant to be good years.

But perhaps the most important dimension of aging well lies in the awareness that there is a purpose to aging. There is a reason for old age, whatever our state of life, whatever our social resources. There is intention built into every stage of life, no less this one than any other. "The evening of a well-spent life," the French moralist Joubert wrote, "brings its lamps with it." Old age enlightens—not simply ourselves, as important as that may be, but those around us as well. Our task is to realize that. In fact, the end-time of life is one of its best, one of its most important. The question is, why?

Who of us hasn't heard it said, over and over, that "we only have one life to live"? Life, the phrase intimates, is to be one unending, unerring line; what we did yesterday, what we do today, cannot be undone. The lifelong implications of this kind of thinking can be deadly. They set the future in cement, they freeze our successes or failures in eternal measures, they short-circuit tomorrow in ways we can never repair. After all, if every act determines the next one, there is no newness, no change. There is only biological time, the inextricable, unending predestination of day after day. What is now determines what is to come.

But I have not found it that way. On the contrary. My life has been nothing but a series of new beginnings.

Now that I am in my seventies I know why I never paid much attention to the notion that life was one continuous extension of yesterday. In fact, the whole idea made me very uncomfortable. It was one of those scoldings that adults insist are not scoldings at all—but which young people detect like bird dogs on the trail. The point was that whatever decision a person made in any particular case would either save or ruin their lives forever. As if "life" were a kind of monochromatic moment of indivisible parts whose future we foreordain by every present piece of it.

The real truth, I have come to think, is that there is no such thing as having only one life to live. The fact is that every life is simply a series of lives, each one of them with its own task, its own flavor, its own brand of errors, its own type of sins, its own glories, its own kind of deep, dank despair, its own plethora of possibilities, all designed to lead us to the same end—happiness and a sense of fulfillment.

Life is a mosaic made up of multiple pieces, each of them full in itself, each of them a stepping-stone on the way to the rest of it.

Most apparent to me now is that each of our separate lives, however much they are part of one continuous lifeline, is discrete. Each of them is distinct, is actually a uniquely apprehensible part of the whole of life. Each of them makes us new. And each of them has a purpose.

First, you master what it is to be alive. You learn to talk and walk and not to spill things or scream too loud or stamp your feet and say "NO!" however much you want to do it anyway.

Then, in the next phase, you learn how to be a student and how to make friends. Or maybe you learn that you can't make friends, that there's just something about you the others don't like. So, in the end you might miss out on the in-crowd. Nevertheless, you manage instead to shape a far steadier clod of self-esteem out of some incorruptible core inside of you that keeps insisting that you are all right no matter who says otherwise. You begin to find a "you" in you.

Finally, you grow up. They pronounce you an adult. And, interestingly enough, you really think you are.

So, you get credentialed in something, either by somebody's institution or by your own apprenticeship to life. You become a salesperson or a manager, the head cook in a diner or a dermatologist, a firefighter or a teacher, a dental assistant or a welder. You have a career, a profession, a skill, a piece of the world on which to mark your presence. You meet someone whose vision of life matches yours, you find a partner who equals your energy in giving it flesh, you start a family and settle in together for long years ahead. Or you opt for the single life, to move around, to see the world, to devote yourself to a career or a ministry. Whatever the case, if you are lucky, you have a goal.

But, often enough, the things you learn about life in this phase get lost in the frenzy of achieving the goal. You struggle to get employed and to stay employed. You get jobs and quit jobs and lose jobs. You exhaust yourself buying the house or getting the degree or creating the security this culture likes to think will last to the end.

Till, unexpectedly, time begins to set in with a vengeance. There are only so many years left now to pay the mortgage.

There are only so many years to plan for retirement. There are a series of downsizings and company closings or, for some perhaps, promotions and bonuses and benchmarks of professional accomplishment.

Then, just as simply as it began, it's over. There's the first pension check, or the senior citizen ticket on the bus. There's retirement—that feeling of freedom which, for many, can just as suddenly turn to feelings of enforced uselessness.

There's the high, gray wall called "the later years."

Academics write scholarly articles about the psychological quality or physical changes of those years. But when we are growing from one phase of our lives to another, all we know is that getting older is just about getting older.

What is the meaning of all of this? "As we grow old we become both more foolish and more wise," the French writer La Rochefoucauld said.

So which one is it? What is the purpose of all these extra years, the ones out of the systems, beyond the corporate institutions. Is this the dying time? Is it only about waiting to be gone? And if so, how can we possibly face it with any kind of joy, any kind of dignity?

I can only be sure of what I see around me. Margaret at ninety-five, once a master seamstress, still goes looking for work. "I'm open for business," she says as she hunts around for new slacks to hem for friends or new drapes to sew. She talks to everyone around her, seeks them out when they miss coming by. She reads and listens to music. She keeps in touch with old pupils. She listens to new lectures on CDs. She lives. There is something about her that sanctifies time, makes it creative rather than stale. She gives me insight into the part of my own life that I cannot yet see. She tells me that life is not measured by years.

Each period of life has its own purpose. This later one gives me the time to assimilate all the others. The task of this period of life, Margaret teaches me, is not simply to endure the coming of the end of time. It is to come alive in ways I have never been alive before.

This book looks at the many dimensions of the aging process, its purpose and its challenges, its struggles and its surprises, its problems and its potential, its pain and its joys. It deals with the sense of rejection that comes from feeling out of touch with the rest of life. It examines the difference between doing and being, and argues that both are important dimensions of life. Both are essential to the fabric of life, both are meant to be gifts to society, not one important and the other insignificant. It looks at the temptation to isolate ourselves from the changes occurring all around us. It looks at what happens to us as our old relationships end and shift, change, and disappear in favor of the many new people and new challenges that come to take their place. It talks about the fear of tomorrow and the mystery of forever. It talks about how to cope with it all. It is a panoply of life issues that emerge with age to bring us to fullness of life, to make us new again.

This is a book not meant to be read in one sitting, or even in order. Like the older years themselves, it is meant to be taken more slowly, more reflectively, more seriously. One topic at a time. It is meant to be read over and over again, if for no other reason than to take the pulse of life as we go on from one issue, one decade, to another.

These are the capstone years, the time in which a whole new life is in the making again. But the gift of these years is not merely being alive—it is the gift of becoming more fully alive than ever.

REGRET

"Do not brood over your past mistakes and failures," the Indian Swami Sivananda wrote, "as this will only fill your mind with grief, regret and depression."

Regret, one of the ghosts of aging, comes upon us one day dressed up like wisdom, looking profound and serious, sensible and responsible. It prods us to begin to look back. It presses us to question everything we've ever done: I should have listened to my mother . . . ; I should have stayed in school . . . ; I should have waited to get married . . . ; I should have majored in something else . . . ; I should have changed jobs . . . ; I should have spent more time with the children, with the family, at home . . . ; I should have gone away from this place, this town, this dull, or wild, or confining life, it whispers.

The exercise is an exhausting one. It is also a dangerous one.

It nibbles around the edges of the mind, and we feel the weariness that comes with it. The years have slipped by without our realizing it. And now it is too late to make the changes regret demands. Too late to take the trip I always dreamed of, too late to get another job, too late to move to the cabin in the woods, too late to go to the big city where everything is surely bigger, brighter, better. Too late to begin again, to do it better this time. Worst of all, regret demands to know why I did what I did in the first place. And I don't know.

This compulsion to look back, to explain to myself, to others, why I did what I did—or, worse, to justify why I didn't do something else—is one of the most direct roads to depression we have. Our thoughts, emotions, and attitudes, according to Dr. Andrew Weil in his book *Healthy Aging*, are "key determinants of how we age." They can threaten the quality of time we bring to the present.

"It's almost over," we hear our hearts say, "and what did we do with the time?" Slowly, stealthily, the past begins to demand as much of our attention as does the present. Sometimes even more.

But it's not only the past that disappoints us when regret begins. The brooding slips over into the present, too. It sours the immediate. It takes the bounce out of our steps. Wherever we are now, whatever we're doing, we could have done something else. Something more satisfying. Something more important. Something more valuable.

Then the notion of past choices—of the things we did not do—begins to damp the glow of what we did do.

The thought of what could have been eats at the center of the heart. It pretends to be reflection, a kind of tally of the years. But down deep it feels more like failure than it does like understanding. What have we made of our lives? What have we become?

We find ourselves beginning to rethink everything we've ever done. Old friends reappear one day, and we begin to judge our lives against theirs. It isn't that we think so much about what they have done as we think about what we ourselves have not done.

The whole effort strikes at the center of our lives with unyielding blows. Why did we do this, not do that, fail to do the other thing? The lights of the soul begin to dim. Life takes on a grayness we have never known before. We put ourselves at the last judgment—and fear our failures.

Regret claims to be insight. But how can it be spiritual insight to deny the good of what has been for the sake of what was not? No, regret is not insight. It is, in fact, the sand trap of the soul. It fails to understand that there are many ways to fullness of life, all of them different, all of them unique.

The exercise of regret looks simple enough, innocent enough to begin with, but there is an immovable quality to it. It drags us down into the center of ourselves, wet and heavy, and leaves us stymied in fantasy. It creates a false life out of gossamer and air, and regrets the one we have. It spends good time on what was not rather than on what is.

Regret is a temptation. It entices us to lust for what never was in the past rather than to bring new energy to our changing present. It is a misuse of the aging process. One of the functions—one of the gifts—of aging is to become comfortable with the self we are, rather than to mourn what we are not. When we devalue it, we bring everything we are and were into question, into doubt. We doubt the God who made us and walks with us all the way to the end.

But the regret that comes with age can also be the very grace we need to connect again with the energy that brought us to this moment in the first place. Regret comes with two faces: to regret our failures is one thing, but to regret our life choices is entirely another.

When we regret the roads that have led us to where we are now, we risk the loss of the future. We drain it of new possibility. We fail to see that these new roads we're on can be just as life-giving, just as good for us, just as full of God-ness as the roads we've come down in the past.

However, when we regret doing what we should never have done—injuring someone's reputation, abusing someone we loved, abandoning the truth for the sake of advancement or approval, violating our own bodies to the point of physical or emotional degradation—we know we have grown into someone of value. It is a moment of great enlightenment when we realize that the years have grown us as well as sustained us. We are of more substance now than we were when we were young, whatever we did in the past, wherever we were when we did it.

The fact is that the twinges of regret are a step-over point in life. They invite us to revisit the ideals and motives that brought us to where we are now. They remind us of the people we loved, the sense of direction that drove us on, the commitments we made and kept. It is the choices we made in the past that have brought us to be the person we are today. The roads not taken may have done the same. But then again, they may not have.

As it is, we can now, clear-eyed and more conscious of what the years did bring us rather than what they did not, understand why we are who we are.

By all means, we must look back. By all means, we must ask ourselves why we are where we are. And we must ask, too, why we did not do all the things we thought, at least at one time, we wanted to do, we should have done.

Those answers, those motives, tell us who we really are. When we rethink our past choices, the central question is if everything in us that needed to develop as a result of each choice, did. Have the lives we chose brought us to the fullness of life God wants for each of us?

The burden of regret is that, unless we come to understand the value of the choices we made in the past, we may fail to see the gifts they have brought us.

The blessing of regret is clear—it brings us, if we are willing to face it head on, to the point of being present to this new time of life in an entirely new way. It urges us on to continue becoming.

MEANING

"It is not by muscle, speed, or physical dexterity that great things are achieved," Cicero wrote over two thousand years ago, "but by reflection, force of character, and judgment." And he goes on, "In these qualities, old age is usually not only not poorer, but is even richer."

Today we live in a world that judges its achievements by speed and busyness. We live in a whirligig of cyberspace communications that smother us in information and data, in international shopping sprees and instant messaging. Time and space, time and thought have very little currency now. It becomes harder by the day to find time to think. Instead of thinking, we do. We are so busy making things happen that we have little time left to think about the value of what is happening.

We urgently need people who concentrate on the meaning of life rather than simply the speed, the mechanization, the computerization of it.

Instead, we have been reduced to a collection of numbers.

Governments and corporations want to know—and file away for posterity—the number of the house or apartment in which we live, the phone number at which we can be reached, the year in which we graduated from school, the number of degrees we have, the number of people in our families, the Social Security number the government has given us by which it will someday, maybe, legitimate our right to be nursed, fed, and housed somewhere in the future—and most important of all, it seems, the number of jobs we've held.

None of those numbers asks us what we think about God, or how we feel about the way the country is going, or whether or not the quality of our lives now is nearly as good as it used to be, or could be, or ought to be. No, they do not want to know our thoughts. They do not care if we have ever baited a hook, saved a dying bird, or devoted our lives to enhancing the quality of life for those around us. They do not ask us what we believe or why, what we would die for or why, what we hope for or why. Clearly, meaning does not seem to be what we are about in our kind of world.

No wonder so many of us feel like pawns on a board, like cogs on a gear. The message we have internalized is clear—we are what we do and what we own, not what we are inside ourselves. Where it counts!

We are in that period of life now where the question that plagues us is the very question that will either destroy or develop us—depending on how we deal with the answer to it. This question, and how we answer it, are central to the last stage of life. We must not only ask ourselves, what are we when we pass from doing to being? For the sake of our happiness and mental health, we must also answer the question:

What am I when I am not what I used to do? And does anybody really care? And what does that have to do with growing into God?

When the job ends or the position disappears or the role outlives itself—when I'm not the moneymaker anymore or the boss anymore, or the councilwoman anymore, or the teacher anymore, or even the parent-in-residence anymore—what does it mean to be alive? In an age when two out of every five workers are forced to stop working earlier than planned, the disorientation has all the characteristics of a social epidemic.[1]

In a society in which people routinely ask what work we do immediately after they ask our name, the question is not simply a philosophical one. In a country with an average retirement age of sixty-four, and a life expectancy of fifteen to twenty years beyond that, the question is a crucial one: *What* am I when I am no longer young enough to strive for a position, to garner another trophy, to get another raise, to race off in the morning to put in hours at the local office of some company? *Who* am I when the job ends and I find myself with barely enough money to pay the rent?

These are the hard questions that come with retirement. These are the nagging questions that make for the tough days of transition from being something to being nothing in a social system in which positions and functions and recognition mean everything. These are the core questions that expose the depth of spirituality in us.

In a hard-driving, action-oriented society, work is everything. Even to use the word "retired" makes employment the center and fulcrum of life.

To survive financially, let alone to get ahead, we have suppressed what we think and what we believe in for so long, it is almost impossible to remember what those thoughts and beliefs were—if we ever really knew. In the interest of civil harmony, we have "gone along" in life rather than take a new way of thinking or living ourselves. Up until this point, it has most of all been more a matter of functioning well than of living well. Oh, we voted, of course, but too often even that great act of moral evaluation was more an act of economic security than a commitment to spiritual principles or to the rest of the human race.

I might have been an effective person, but not always a spiritual person. And now that effectiveness is no longer the driving feature of my life, what am I?

With years ahead of me now, what can I do to avoid the hollowness within that comes with the stripping away of all the accoutrements of life that go with a job? Like the cocktail parties for the staff, or the company picnics for the families, or the holiday letters that detail all my successes to my friends.

This is the time of coming home to the self. I find myself stripped of all the accessories of life now. I am face-to-face with my self. And the fear is that there isn't one. I have spent my life being somebody important, and now there is nothing left but me. I no longer run anything, I'm not becoming anything. I'm just me now. And what is that?

Meaning—the message of my life, the substance of my being—is left standing there, bare and shivering, once all the titles and perks are gone. I'm me. Just me.

What do the others see in me now? What does God see in me now? What do I see in myself now? What am I doing with my time now? What gets me out of bed in the morning that is greater than the discomfort of staying in it?

That is really the great question of older age in the Western world. What *am* I when I'm nothing else? What's left over of me when everything else goes: the positions, the power, the status, the job, the goal, the role, the impact—and all the relationships built up and woven around those things? "Out of the depths I cry to you, O God," the psalmist wept. And now there is a psalmist in all of us.

The answer to such overwhelming questions is a complicated one. Of course I am all the experiences I have ever had, on one level. But on another level, I am only what people see when they look at me now. Finally, I am only what I have prepared myself to be beyond what I did. And what is that?

The world has been upside down for so long, it is almost impossible to believe anymore that the meaning of life is *not* about doing. The notion that it is about *being*—being caring, being interested, being honest, being truthful, being available, being spiritual, being involved with the important things of life, of living—is so rare, so unspoken of, as to be obtuse. We don't even know what meaning means anymore.

But one thing is sure: to be meaningful to the world around us means that we need to provide something more than numbers. It means that we are obliged to offer important ideas, sacred reflection, a serious review of options, and the suggestion of better ideas than the ones the world is running on now. It means that we prod the people around us to reflect on what they themselves are doing—while they can still change it. It is about what we strive to do because it is worth doing, because it is God's will for the world.

Taking care of a neighbor who is far more limited than I am gives me something to think about other than myself. Dedicating myself to the local school as a teacher's aide involves me in the development of the next generation. Creating a discussion group to explore the effects of legislation on people of all classes in my city makes me a thinking member of a thinking population. Being a patron of the arts in the region maintains its cultural soul. Joining a government watchdog group in the city brings wisdom to the art of politics. Becoming the one in every group who asks the others more than just, "And what do you do for a living?" might even be the very thing that gives spiritual meaning to their lives as well.

Cicero was right. The older generation has a great deal to give the world. But first, they must come to value it themselves.

A burden of these years is that we might allow ourselves to believe that not being as fast or as busy as we used to be is some kind of human deficiency.

A blessing of these years is that we can come to understand that it is the quality of what we think and say that makes us valuable members of society, not how fast or busy we are.

FEAR

"Age is not all decay," George MacDonald said. "It is the ripening, the swelling, of the fresh life within that withers and bursts the husk."

It is not the getting older that is difficult. It is the fear of getting older that plagues us. Instead of seeing a long life as a gateway to the flowering of the spirit, the growing of the soul, we are far more likely in a culture geared toward movement and dexterity, physical beauty and public achievement, to see it as the coming of a wasteland. We need to think again about the beauties of age, its freedom and its splendor. It is the "fresh life within" that age reveals to us, if we only give it a chance. It is learning to give new challenges a chance that make the later years a spiritual adventure as well as a psychological stumbling block. Some of us meet its demands with the joy of the climb. Others are more disposed to move in place. It is the difference between life and non-life, between seeing a beckoning God everywhere and coming to the end of the search.

When she ventured out of the house that day, the wind was

sharp and the air was crisp. The sight of the glowing weir at the top of the grade, high and fast flowing, invited walkers deeper and deeper into the wooded area beyond it. "You'll have to walk faster than that," the man on the footpath behind her said, "if you want to keep warm here today. Up there at the weir it will be even colder."

"Oh," the woman said, "I'm not going all the way to the weir. That's a bit far for me." She smiled the polite smile women in their late sixties, early seventies, do so well.

"Really," the man said as he hurried on. "Well, I'm eighty-seven, and if I do it every day," and he tipped his hat as he went, "surely you can."

There are those, of course, for whom physical loss is a major feature of the aging process. But actually far fewer than we are inclined to think. According to the Longitudinal Study on Aging and the National Health Interview Survey, rates of disability are declining steadily, and recovery from acute disabilities improves from year to year. The ratio of active to dependent life expectancy—of healthy old age as opposed simply to length of years—is increasing at rates unheard of before this time. If anything, the elderly are the fastest-growing segment of the modern population.[2]

In 2005, data shows, only seven percent of those between seventy-five and eighty-four, and only twenty-five percent of those over eighty-four, needed help with personal care.[3]

Evidence also tells us that decrepitude and incapacitation that come with age are, on average, only about the last three months of a life.[4] Even then, studies assure us, mental clarity is more likely than not to remain to the end. Clearly, life does not end till it ends.

We have, without doubt, a lot of life left to live. Which means, of course, that we have a lot of responsibility as well. The major question facing us now is, how will we live it? Will we live it as a kind of dark and slowly dying time where life is one long list of perpetual endings? Or will we live it as an entirely new stage of life, meant both to challenge us and to develop a maturity, a mellowness, of personality and character that makes us not only acceptable but even necessary to those around us? Sought after, in fact!

Indeed, we are at a crossroads now, in the starkest kind of way. We are at the point in life where we must make the kind of decisions that will determine the quality of our remaining years.

When we count age as nothing but a series of losses, we lose sight of its gains. Then, a natural kind of fear invades the soul of a person. It is always there. It shadows us. It lies inside us like the tick of a clock in the heart. It warns of the time when we will not be as lithe, as steady, as we have always known ourselves to be.

When the first pain comes, when the knee, we suddenly realize, has become tender without warning, we shrug it off as some kind of injury we do not remember. "An old football injury," maybe. Or a moment while I gardened "when the ground was harder than I thought."

But slowly, slowly, reality sets in: this is the first sign of impending arthritis; it is the first symptom of joint damage; the first sure warning of a creeping, an insidious, physical change. In me. The strong one. The one who has never been sick before, who has walked the steps all the time. The one who has stayed fit or stayed active or stayed healthy forever—till now.

Then, what I fear is not the pain, but the sure and obvious signal that the self I was is changing. No, correction. It is deteriorating.

I find myself listening more intently than I ever had before to other people's medical reports. I compare them to my own. My arthritis is not as bad as theirs, is the same as theirs, is worse than theirs. Other people's bodies become the measure of my own vitality, of the vibrancy of the life force within me.

Most of all, though, I begin to count years. "How old was she when she died?" I ask. "What did she die from?" I want to know. How much older is she than I am?

The questions never end. The concentration narrows to things I never thought of before. How do I feel, I now ask myself every morning.

But underneath it all, the questions are not physical at all. They are emotional, psychological, social ones, spiritual ones. What did I really think my existence was all about if not about coming to the end of this life, and coming to the beginning of another? What have I done in the past to come confidently to this moment? What can I do now to finally become what I have been meant to be? And all of those questions come out of fear. How much longer will I be able to take care of myself? Who will take care of me when I can't do it anymore? And, the major one: Is my life over now? Is there nothing left of the me I have always been? Is life now only to be endured rather than lived? And, of course, which dimension of life have I not lived well up to until this time? What can I do about that now, if I am ever to be the person I was meant to be?

Too often, we fail to realize that this very fear in us may be the best sign of life we have. It means, ironically, that we are very much alive. In the twentieth century, life expectancy nearly doubled. The French call the time after retirement "the third age." And there will be a great deal of it. In 1992, twelve percent of the population of the United States was over sixty-five. By 2020, demographers tell us, eighteen percent of the country will be over sixty-five. Obviously, life after sixty-five is not a pathology. It is a whole new look at what life can be at this stage of it.[5]

The major task of life in this period may simply be not to fear the fear. Every sign of change in me, the very things I fear to lose, are a call for new beginnings. If I have lost the energy, the ability, to walk long distances, for example, then I must find something to do that I will love just as passionately, learn from just as deeply. Maybe it's collecting all my favorite concertos on CD. Maybe it's studying a new language in preparation for a trip to another part of the world. Maybe it's watching the birds at a feeder on my window. Maybe this is the time to really figure out what computers are all about. Perhaps it is about paying attention to the part of me that is beyond the physical, more than the physical, free of the physical.

One thing this period is *not* about is diminishment, though physical diminishment is surely a natural part of it. It is, instead, about giving ourselves over to a new kind of development, to the kinds of change that began in us at the time of conception and continue in us still. The truth is that we are a great deal more than our bodies, have always been more than our bodies, but it can take us most of a lifetime to learn that. Our moral obligation is not, as society might lead us to believe, to ski at sixty and jog at seventy and bike at eighty. No, our moral obligation is to stay as well as we can, to remain active, to avoid abusing our bodies, to do the things that interest us and to enrich the lives of those around us. Our spiritual obligation is to age well—so that others who meet us may have the courage, the spiritual depth, to do the same. Abandoning life before life is over is not just resignation; it is not trying to reach for God on God's terms.

Aging well does not mean that we will not change physically. But it does mean that we will not define ourselves only by our continuing physical proficiencies.

This is the time to begin to think of higher matters than looking ten years younger than we are, wonderful as that can be. We must begin to attend to the inner self now. These years are for allowing the interior life—our continuing questions, our lifelong interests—to direct what we do and who we are.

This is the time to put soil and seeds in a pot and grow something. We have the hours now to tend and water it. We have time to be patient.

This is the time for reconnecting with the part of the family we haven't seen or heard from for years.

This is the time to embrace the world as a whole, to care about the starving in Africa and the illiterate in the Middle East and the poor in our own neighborhood.

But whatever we do, we must do it consciously. We must do it knowing that for all the losses, there are new things to gain as well.

What we must not do is do nothing. We cannot allow ourselves to die from the outside in. It may be necessary to live with a body that is changing. That we can't avoid. But the shape of our life itself we can control. We are responsible for the shape of our world, however much it seems to be reshaping itself.

Why should we bother? Because the generations around us depend on us as much as we depend on them. We depend on them for the cosmetics of life, its inventions and institutions and products. They depend on us, on the older generation, to give them a spiritual model, a psychological archetype of how to live it.

Life always comes out of death. The present rises from the ashes of the past. The future is always possible for those who are willing to re-create it.

The task of every separate stage of life is to confront its fears so that it can become more than it was. For the young, it is overcoming the fear of functioning alone. For the middle-aged, it is dealing with the fear of failure. For those of us who have moved beyond the middle years, it is learning to cope with the fear of weakness.

A burden of these years is the possibility of giving in to the fear of invisibility, of uselessness, of losing our sense of self and human obligation. Fear tempts us to believe that life is over—rather than simply changing.

A blessing of fear in these years is that it invites us to become the fullness of ourselves. It comes to us in the nighttime of the soul to tell us to rise to new selves in fresh and exciting ways—for our sake, of course, but for the sake of the rest of the world, as well.

AGEISM

"I am sixty-five and I guess that puts me in with the geriatrics," James Thurber remarked. "But if there were fifteen months in every year, I'd only be forty-eight. That's the trouble with us: We number everything."

To be over sixty-five in an age like ours is to feel bad even when we feel good. We are, after all, "old" now. Except, we don't feel "old." And we don't think "old." And we work very hard at not looking "old"—whatever looking old is supposed to mean. But, oh, we have been taught to mind "old." We're too old to get a job, they tell us—but they want us to volunteer all the time. We're too old to drive a car, they fear—but there are proportionally far more automobile accidents caused by drivers between the ages of eighteen and twenty-five than by drivers over sixty-five. We're too old to get health insurance—but we haven't been seriously ill for years.

Which leads us to the larger question, the real question: what difference does it make how wise we are, how well we are, how alert we are, how involved we are after we're sixty-five? After all, once you reach retirement age in this culture, everything is canceled. We're "old" now, and we know it. And the rest of the world knows it, too. We're "old"—translate "useless," translate "unwanted," translate "out of place," translate "incompetent." We are the over-the-hill gang, our birthday cards say. And we laugh—as well as we can—but, if truth were known, the laugh comes with a stab in the psyche.

We wince when we watch television. There we are in living color. Who could possibly like or want to identify with so much of what we see? Older characters on television are not the philosophers of our age, the sages or medicine women of past times. No, the elderly of our time are portrayed as frail and bumbling creatures who dodder along doing nothing, understanding nothing, aware of nothing, muttering. They're "away with the fairies," as the Irish say.

Those representations are not true, and we know that, too, because we're it, we're the real thing. And we do not bumble or dodder or mutter. We think very well, thank you, and we work hard and we know precisely what is going on in the world around us. But what good does that do in a culture that begins to eliminate its experienced workers at the age of fifty-five on the basis of a stereotype which does not hold up under scrutiny, but which is very difficult to change?

Negative stereotypes exaggerate isolated characteristics and ignore positive characteristics entirely. So older people are portrayed as slow, but not as wise or patient. We see them as ill, but not as quite in charge of their own lives. We are reminded constantly that they forget things, but not a single note is made of the fact that everyone else does as well.

Worst of all, stereotypes absolutize characteristics, as if they were part and parcel of being black or being a woman or being old—or of being young, for that matter. We group people together, instead of seeing them as individuals who are full of grace, full of the spirit of life. We allow no chance for change, and so a stereotyped group begins to think of itself like this, too.

It is a pathetic moment in the history of the human condition when the outside world tells us who and what we are—and we start to believe it ourselves. Then, bent over from the weight of the negativity, we start to wither on the outside, just as we have already begun to wither within. The pace slows, the interest dims, the energy for life fades and fails.

But don't be fooled. Most of us, as Dylan Thomas said, go toward the end of life, raging "against the dying of the light."

Ed, in his late eighties, went to the club every day of his life, but only after he had finished at least nine holes of golf. Bus, in his seventies, played cards every afternoon and told jokes all afternoon as he did. Kathleen, almost ninety, worked in different charitable agencies everywhere, day after day, because everybody wanted her and none of them could do without her. Tim, over eighty, was the highest-rated volunteer in Meals on Wheels, organizing and delivering more meals a day than any other younger worker in the system. Ted, in his high seventies, a university trustee and once a banker and a financial manager, acted as a consultant to nonprofit agencies in an attempt to enable them to achieve some kind of viability. No stereotype here. These elders were alive socially, engaged publicly, necessary to the community in which they lived.

The point is, we are the only icons of aging that younger people will get to meet. What we show them as we go, gives them a model of what they, too, can strive for. We show them the way to the fullness of life.

For years now, researchers have known that only five percent of those over sixty-five are in special-care institutions, and eighty percent of the rest of the older population have no limitations in managing the rigors of daily living.[6] With the rise of online shopping and banking services, that number is getting even larger by the day. And yes, more older people than younger ones have chronic illnesses, but they also have fewer acute illnesses than younger ones. They have fewer injuries in the home and also have fewer accidents on the highway. And with the new emphasis on gerontology, these rates are decreasing as well.[7]

Even the notion of physical beauty depends more on what we truly see, rather than what we're just looking at. In Japan, for instance, silver hair and wrinkles are valued as signs of wisdom and service.[8] In the West, walking a lot is a sign of vigor at any age. In other cultures, age alone—rather than physical attributes—gives social privilege. Obviously, physical attractiveness is culturally specific, not universal. Older people are just as physically attractive as younger people, but different cultures define the meaning of "attractive" in different ways.

Finally, most older people retain their normal mental abilities, including short-term memory, their entire lives. They are just as able to learn and remember as younger people, though they begin to process information differently, and they may take longer to complete a project. Chronological age, however entrenched the stereotypes of its importance peddled on birthday cards, cartoons, and situation comedies may be, does not have a major influence on learning.[9]

This and so much other scientific data—the reliability and acuity of older workers, the rarity of mental illness among the elderly, the vibrancy of their emotional relationships as well as their capacity for sexual relations—has been known in the academic community for years now. It is tested over and over, and the findings both remain stable and become even stronger as a new generation of older people claim their natural right to live till they die.

What we may be forgetting in the light of such facts is that these gifts of aging well are not without spiritual meaning. "To those to whom much has been given," we know, "much is expected"—and that means us, too. Age does not forgive us our responsibility to give the world back to God a bit better than it was because we were here.

All the old jokes about old people are fast wearing thin now. Ageism is a lie. The only way to counter it, however, is to refuse to allow it to taint our own lives. Age is not a thing to be pitied, to apologize for, to fear, to resist, to see as a sign of doom. Only the old can make age a bright and vibrant place to be. And so we must. If we don't, we stand to waste a full twenty-five to thirty percent of our lives. And waste is always a pity.

A burden of these years is the danger that we might internalize the negative stereotypes of the aging process. We might become what we fear, and so abdicate our new call in life.

A blessing of these years is that we are the ones whose responsibility it is to prove the stereotypes wrong, to give age its own fullness of life.

JOY

"As for old age," Seneca said, "embrace and love it. It abounds with pleasure if you know how to use it. The gradually declining years are among the sweetest in life. . . . Even when they have reached the extreme limit they have their pleasure still."

There is something about being free of the expectations and deadlines, pressures and responsibilities, schedules and public activities of the middle years that put the later years of life in a totally different light. There is space now and time. There is possibility now and the kind of accent on people, rather than projects, that we haven't known for years. There is a sense of freshness in these years that speaks a foreign language to the heart.

But Seneca emphasized, "If you know how to use it." That's the important part. Knowing what to do with this new sense of time and space is what determines in the end just how happy, how fulfilling those years will be. And so few of us, creatures of a hard-driving, work-ridden society, really do know.

"Did you hear that we're both retiring next month?" she said. Her voice was tight; the words were strained. She was troubled and too embarrassed to admit it. "I don't know what I'm going to do when we're together all the time," she said, affecting a light laugh after a long, troubled pause. "What do we do now? Sit around and look at one another?"

The worry is a common one. In a society that is productivity-centered, what happens to life once the regular routine ends? What happens to us as people because it ends? We haven't been home together all day every day for years. The very idea can turn the preretirement months into a quiet kind of personal agony. We put on a brave face, but inside the insecurity rages. What will we do now when we get up in the morning? If this is retirement, who needs it? Why go on living when there's nothing left to live for anymore?

Once the great retirement trip is done and over—what do we do then?

All of a sudden we find ourselves faced with what we thought was supposed to be the acme of life, the pinnacle of it. But when we look down from it now, there's nothing there.

The realization that, after all these years, all we know to do is to work comes thundering down into the center of us. And the center is empty.

We find ourselves at the greatest moment of choice we've ever had, at least since we left home on our own, since we identified what we wanted to do in life, since we made the first great career move, since we decided, finally, to settle down. Now we have to decide how to live without being told how it's done.

The slate is clean. The days are ours. The task now is to learn how to live again.

We can decide to live with joy. Or we can allow ourselves to live looking back with bitterness. We can be bitter about all the things we wanted to do, but felt too constrained to risk. We can be bitter for all the hours we gave to a company that was able to say goodbye to us, without so much as remembering to send a card at Christmastime. We can be bitter because we chose security and independence rather than depth and companionship. We can decide to be bitter because at the end, only the end is left. But whichever we decide—bitterness or joy—decide we must. The rest of our life depends on it.

It can take a while before we begin to realize that retirement really plunges us into joy.

But if we decide to live this new, unscripted time with joy, then life will come pouring into us, almost more fully than we can sometimes bear.

This is the period of life of which the psalmist spoke when he prayed, "O taste and see that our God is sweet. . . ."

What we have been doing all these years was part of God's will for life. It was all meant for something. It was everything we needed at that time to become a full human being. It was indeed, we know now, very, very sweet. And so is this time now—and for the very same reason. Long life is part of the will of God for us.

This is the period for allowing ourselves to rejoice in the past that brought us to this point, as well as to revel in the possibilities that are the present.

There are lessons to be learned from life before this period that will serve us still—if we will only attend to them. We have every right to live in gratitude for all the stages of life that brought us here, for the memories that give us great joy, the people who helped us get this far, the accomplishments we carved on our hearts along the way. These experiences cry out to be celebrated. They are no more past than we are. They live in us forever.

They merit a loving smile, a happy laugh, a bittersweet tear or two as well. We can be proud of where we've been, what we conquered as we grew, what we became in the doing of it.

We need to allow these experiences to wash through us again, this time not so much for the circumstances we remember as for the insights they bring, the warmth they give us yet. These are the experiences that had meaning to us then, and there is meaning in them yet to be sucked out, to be savored—differently, of course, but still.

We can be full of joy, too, because we have come to this moment of new freedom. Now, heads up and alert, we can examine every possibility and decide for the first time, perhaps, what we really want to do with life, rather than what we must do, or should do, or ought to do. We have the joy of immunity from propriety now. Like children on a beach, we can decide whether we will wear sandals or go barefoot through life from now on.

Most of all, we can decide to walk gently through this last great stage of life when everything begins to come together for us, to make sense, to have new meaning.

We can simply sit and watch a sunset, since we are not rushing home through traffic as the sun goes down.

We can walk across the lawn in the morning dew, smell the grass and pick a dandelion, because, like the glorious rose, it has a beauty all its own, as do all things, if we will only learn to look for it.

We can be happy to be seventy, to be where we've been, to

know what we know, to have today to do even more. We can begin to make creation the spirit of our spirit and, this time, breathe it in slowly so it saturates our heart and enables us to see the parts of creation we have failed to see before this moment of our lives.

We can decide to smile at everyone we meet, to play with children, to talk to seniors, to ask questions of youngsters—and this time to listen to their answers.

We can determine to pursue something new today, become a learner again, and feel the excitement that begins to rise in us when we do.

We can decide to give ourselves to those who have no one else but us to count on for quality of life themselves.

Now we have it all: opportunity, freedom, and the sense to know what those things demand of us. We have a chance to be the best self we have ever been. And we have the chance to help others do the same.

A burden of these years is to fail to get beyond the bitterness of having been displaced, and to not see that being moved quietly off all the platforms of life is also to be free of the stagecraft that goes with them.

A blessing of these years is to wake up one morning and find ourselves drunk with the very thought of being alive. Then, wherever we go we will spread the joy we have finally been able to find in ourselves.

AUTHORITY

"Old age, especially an honored old age," Cicero said, "has so great authority, that this is of more value than all the pleasure of youth."

The idea is a far cry from today's prevailing notion of the worthlessness of anything old, not new, not fresh off the vine. So engrained is the concept of newness nowadays that every year what we call "old" gets younger and the obsolete gets newer.

The idea of deliberate obsolescence has been with us for several decades now. Alvin Toffler's *Future Shock* first introduced the concept of "planned obsolescence" in the 1970s. Then the public discovered that automobile tires would hold up for only so many miles, that companies could predict with startling accuracy just how long a refrigerator motor would last, that light bulbs would operate for a predictable number of hours. The pride of the maker lay no longer in the fact that you could use a product for years. Instead, things were meant to be eliminated. Most things were timed to end. Nothing was made to last anymore. Upgrades were the thing now. New-ness made the world go round, not longevity, not quality. The economy depended on it.

The problem is that it came to be applied to people, too. In this kind of a culture we are all in danger of becoming obsolete quickly. In this kind of a technological society the growing margination of older persons is all too obvious.

In most societies, the elderly have been revered. In many cultures, only the elderly were considered fit to rule. They were the members of the community who were responsible for guiding everybody's future because they had more knowledge about living, about history, about the memory of the group than all the others. More than that, they also had the benefit of years to help them show the younger members of the community how to live well after them.

Modern society, on the other hand, so often spins leaders through a revolving door of defined term limits and moves on. This is a culture that cannot afford old age. We are long past looking for ripened experience. The more removed any of us is from the latest findings in the technological or scientific fields, we presume, the less he or she is qualified to be a leader. It isn't the wisdom that comes from years of growing into something that we want anymore, it's new information that counts. Then, all too quickly, we find ourselves outmoded by those who take that data and quickly move beyond it—and us.

And that is precisely one of the major problems with growing older in this society. Of what use are we now? What do we do but sit on the sundeck, or walk the streets, or hole up in a high-rise building alone and wait till it's over? Where is Cicero's authority of age now that is "of more value than all the pleasure of youth?"

It is difficult, indeed, to find the value of experience honored or preserved, sought after and revered in such a world as this.

But old age is not for nothing—or there wouldn't be any. Clearly, old age has a role to play in the development of the world around us. We do not live all these later years simply not to die. We live in order to make life better—both for ourselves and for others. But how?

Transition from public functionary to public figure, from institutional foot soldier to independent philosopher at large, is an important one, but it is also a difficult one. One problem is that, unlike in so many other cultures, this figure of wisdom has no name in our society.

In many indigenous cultures, it is the shaman—the wizened medium between the visible and the spirit world. The shamans are the experts in the folklore of a culture and, in most shamanic cultures, have had lengthy training in it. They understand the world they live in. They have delved into it deeply.

In Judaism, such a figure is the tzaddik, the "righteous one," the one who over the years has achieved outstanding piety, the one who is a sign to every other Jew of how to live, "a leader of the generation."

In Hinduism, the one who embarks on the spiritual quest after retirement is the sanyasi, whose example of the final great quest is legend in the society.

In Buddhism, the one who puts off personal nirvana to work for the enlightenment of the rest of the world is called the bodhisattva. In this person is embodied the best the culture has to offer, the sign of what it is to become better people as we age.

In these cultures there is an understanding that in the older generations resides insight that is lacking to the younger ones.

But what is this insight? Where does it come from? And most important of all, what do we do with insight now?

In every generation there is an accumulated amount of experience which says something about life that is, at the same time, both unique and universal. It comes from the simple act of living a recollected, a reflective life. It comes from having used every dimension of life to prepare for the next one. It comes from living what Socrates had in mind when he said, "The unexamined life is not worth living." The sage, the shaman, the tzaddik, the sanyasi, the bodhisattva, the "elder" are those who, after a lifetime of living, examine what life means. More than that, they set out to pass it on to those who will come after them.

And they have a right to do it. They have the authority of experience, the authority of survival, the authority of persistence, and finally, the responsibility to give the authority of example.

As part of his eighty-ninth birthday celebration, Nelson Mandela announced the creation of "The Elders," a group of "wise men and women." This council of former presidents, elder statesmen, Nobel laureates, and international leaders—among them Mary Robinson, Kofi Annan, Jimmy Carter, and Archbishop Desmond Tutu—will meet twice a year to consider global issues and offer both their expertise and their guidance to current leaders and political figures. Free of the dailiness of past positions, they bring detachment, wisdom, and the long view of personal history relieved of political ambitions or national pressures to current situations. Mandela explained his commitment to the creation of the group. "I am trying to take my retirement seriously," he said. It is a model to be considered in more than the political arena.

Experience is what gives an older person the right to bring, not biography, but history to the situation at hand. The historical memory of a group says, no, going into World War II and the invasion of Vietnam were *not* the same thing. You may support both if you want to, but don't think of them as equal.

Survival is what gives an older person the right to encourage a younger generation in the right to hope, to know that what is happening to them at the present moment is not the end either of the world or of their lives. There is always a resurrection in each our lives, if we will only believe in it and give ourselves to its coming.

Past persistence, even in the face of difficulty, is what allows the older person—who seems to be so far removed from the present situation—to insist that quitting is not the answer to anything. Persistence may not solve everything—at least in our lifetime—but it is truer to the meaning of life for us to wait for another plowing, another seeding, another harvest, than not.

This is the spiritual strength of the elders in every generation. It is our responsibility as well.

When the young look to the stars of their lives to determine in which direction to steer their own, we will have lost a most precious moment if it is not to the wisdom figures of our own generation that they turn. If we do not become "the elders" of our time, what was the spiritual purpose of all our earlier years? Will the world remember the amount of money we made or saved or spent? Will the world enshrine our medals and our plaques? *Or* will a younger generation remember what our own lives said to them about experience, survival, and persistence, about living in such a way that their own mortality has meaning?

A burden of these years is the temptation to consider ourselves obsolete, and to waste this precious time only on ourselves. It is the temptation for ultimate narcissism.

A blessing of these years is our involvement in the important questions of the present, so that the time to come will be more blessed than our own—because of the insights we both preserve in ourselves and pass on to others before we go.

TRANSFORMATION

"I am luminous with age," Meridel Le Sueur wrote. Her words give us pause, make us think, call us to the bar of judgment.

The truth is that older people tend to come in two flavors—the sour ones and the serene ones. The sour ones are angry at the world for dismissing them from the rank and file of those who run it and control it and own it and are not old in it. They demand that the rest of the world seek them out, pity them, take their orders, stay captive to their scowls.

The serene ones live with soft smiles on their aging faces, a welcome sign to the world of what it means to grow old gracefully. To have the grace of old age. They require us to go on growing more and more into ourselves as we age. It is of these that Meridel Le Sueur, who lived to be ninety-six, wrote, "I am luminous with age." Luminous. Not painted. Not masked. Luminous! They are the women and men who see with wider eyes, hear with tuned ears, speak with a more knowing tongue. These are people with soul.

Fashion and fitness magazines are very clear about what seventy is expected to look like these days. "Seventy" is people on exercise machines and in ballroom dance courses. People in their seventies now are walkers and bowlers, swimmers and bikers. They fish and golf, they join choral groups, and play cards. These are people who are trim and full of life, mentally sharp and healthy. They exude vigor and excitement. They go to all the right places, see all the right people, do all the right things. And they never tire while they're doing it. They live life with gusto and panache. They defy the years of their lives and go into the sunset singing and dancing.

And that's true, at least to some degree, for many. Never has a generation before us lived so long or lived so well as in the affluent West. Never has life seemed more eternal than now.

At the same time, there is another physical reality going on. Reading the telephone book without glasses has us squinting now—and we buy reading glasses at the pharmacy. We turn the volume up on the television set higher than we ever did before. We find ourselves noticing hair coloring ads now. And though we do walk a bit every day, we don't go as far—and definitely not as fast—as we did years ago.

There have been changes in life that came unbidden but decisively. There is no going back now—and we know it. We don't say it, of course. We hug it to our breasts like a great gray secret. But we *do* know it. Down deep inside ourselves we know that there is something different going on now. We are being transformed.

But the essential transformation that comes with age is a great deal more than physical well-being, a lot more than being able to play a regular round of golf, an entire way of life different from a Wednesday game of bridge or the weekly round of the clubs.

There is an important part of the aging process that lies in simply getting accustomed to being older. Part of being a vigorous older person demands, first of all, that we learn to accept it for what it is, a new and wonderful—but different—stage of life. We must admit, even in our own minds, to being older in a culture that is so youth-centered that age is something to be hidden, rather than celebrated.

"Me?" we say. "Seventy? Impossible." One can almost hear the tone of shame that goes with it. It burrows into the center of us, and an alarm sounds in the heart. How could life be almost over, we worry, when we were just beginning to understand it, to enjoy it, to love it? And with the fear of age, if we succumb to the notion that being older is some kind of obstacle to life, comes the loss of one of life's most profound periods.

The problem is that preparation for aging in our modern world seems to be concentrated almost entirely on buying anti-wrinkle creams and joining a health club—when the truth is that what must be transformed now is not so much the way we look to other people, as it is the way we look at life. Age is the moment we come to terms with ourselves. We begin to look inside ourselves. We begin to find more strength in the spirit than in the flesh.

The way we view ourselves changes from period to period in life. It is not a steady-state experience, and its most impacting definition comes in middle age. Then, we all get some kind of power, however limited it may be, just by virtue of seniority, if nothing else. We find ourselves in charge somewhere: in charge of the children, in a position of control on the job, in a position of preferment in the family, at a higher social level in the group. We have arrived.

But all of a sudden it seems, as quietly as I arrived, I am now just as quietly dismissed. Power and control cannot be my definition of self anymore. I must now find in myself whatever it is that gives me a personal place in the world around me: I'm fun to be with; I care about other people; I have begun to live for deeper, richer, more important things than I have ever done before. I am caretaker, public watchdog, social advocate, companion now. I begin to see myself differently now. I begin to discover that, in many ways, I am far more important now than I have been all my previous life.

I begin to see the world differently, too. It is to be treasured, to be explored, to be enjoyed. An evening on the beach as the sun goes down is worth all the cocktail parties I've ever attended.

Other people begin to look different to me, too. They are as transformed as I am. I no longer see them as roles. They are people now, individuals—not problems, not "connections," not a measure of my own value. My value now rests entirely in me, in what kind of person I am with others.

I find, too, that the number of absolutes in my life is precipitously reduced. I'm a lot less dogmatic now about the nature of God. I'm not as sure as I once was about what is gravely damning and what is not. Most important of all, I am happy to put that decision in the hands of the God whose nature seems far more compassionate now—as I have gotten more compassionate myself.

Finally, I now see life newly, too. Once I thought of it as a kind of major-league competition for money and status and things. Now I see it as something to value for itself. I begin to realize that it is not about having much—it is about having enough. I begin to understand that the tragedy of life is that so many have so little that even just having enough to live on is beyond them. I begin to understand that there's something wrong with that. I have had more than enough help in life. And what about these others? What is my responsibility to them now?

It is the moment of final and full transformation. I have become the fullness of myself, but only once I was able to put down the cosmetics of the self, like the titles, the privileges, the symbols, and the signs of being something more than I was—and at the same time less than I was.

A burden of these years is the possibility that I might stay more buried in my losses than aware of my gains.

A blessing of these years is the transformation of the self to be, at long last, the self I have been becoming all my life—an oasis of serenity in a world gone sour on age, the very acme of life.

NEWNESS

"Grow old along with me!" Robert Browning wrote. "The best is yet to be, the last of life, for which the first was made."

It's a heady idea, this notion of an excursion into newness just when we begin what we know will certainly be the last major period of our life. The only thing left to discover now, we assume, is when it will be over, when it will finally end. And how.

But that is at best a very narrow view of life. It disregards the nature of life completely. The truth is that life goes on happening, even when we try to avoid it.

We think we'll never move out of the house we're in—and then the roof leaks or the basement floods or we simply cannot walk that long, high flight of stairs anymore. And so we move to somewhere new, somewhere without the past to hold us down.

We think we've "retired"—and then before long all the people in town who need help, who need a consultant, who need a companion, who need a committee member, who need fresh energy, discover that we're available now, free now, and we find ourselves busier than ever.

We think we'll be alone the rest of our lives—and then there's a first meeting, followed by a conversation, followed by dinner four times a week. And life begins to laugh inside of us again. We have someone to talk to, another time to tell the stories, a new desire to listen, the adventure of being heard. Really heard.

Life changes. It is of the essence of life to change. It is of the spiritual character of life to make demands, to bring new challenges, to goad us into living it.

But that life changes is not the issue. Change is obvious. It will come whether we like it or not. Whether we admit it or not. Whether we want it or not. That's simply obvious, too. The real issue is far more subtle than that.

It is not change that will destroy us. It is the attitude we take to it that will make all the difference. The frame of mind we bring to it gives meaning to the end of one phase of life, of course. But more than that, it also determines the spiritual depth with which we start this new phase.

It all comes down to whether we see our existence now as having meaning for others, as well as for ourselves, or simply as a kind of enforced pause between the end of the life that has already happened and the end of the body which will surely happen soon.

The truth is that this new stage of life liberates in a way no other stage of growth can possibly do. All the striving is over now. We don't have to prove ourselves anymore. We don't have to have the way we spend our time approved anymore. We don't have to work, produce, provide, or get ahead anymore. The only thing required of us now is the blooming of the self. Like autumn flowers, rich in color, deep in tone, sturdy in the wind, our lives not only have new color, they bring with them the kind of interior depth a fast-moving world so dearly needs.

If we decide that life is over once the accoutrements of middle age are over—the career, the title, the children, the climb up the social ladder—and that there is nothing else worth doing, that the very definition of who we are has been summarily foreclosed, then of course it will be. We have ended ourselves.

But if we can bring ourselves to strike out now to try on the rest of ourselves, there is a whole new world ahead of us. Parts of ourselves that have been so carefully hidden from others during all the years of responsibility and productivity—and just as often as not hidden from ourselves as well—are now ours for the trying.

And it is the willingness, the eagerness to try, that makes all the difference.

Growth in old age requires the curiosity of a five-year-old and the confidence of a teenager. There is nothing we can't do if we want to do it. We can learn another language, we can walk the city from one end to the other, we can go up and down the street, introduce ourselves to our neighbors and offer to bake a cake for them once a week if they'd like it.

Or we can start a car service for parents who spend their own nights after work driving their children back and forth to band practice and basketball and gymnastic lessons and dental appointments.

We can start a monthly book club and rotate the discussions and buffets that follow them from house to house—so that everybody in the group gets company.

We can lead tour groups, become a local history buff, join every adult education class in town.

We can, in other words, be whatever we want to be now—without the frills, without the protocol, without the posturing. We can re-create ourselves in order to be creative in the world in a different way than the boundaries of our previous life allowed.

And what if we don't want to do anything too involved? Then, of course, we can simply enjoy. There's nothing wrong with leisure if it is steeped in purpose and enrichment. With good music, or good reading, or good walking, or good conversation. But at the same time, we must ask ourselves what is it in us now that makes us want to retreat from the kind of life we have so recently been living? The younger people are when they retire, researchers tell us,[10] the more difficult the transition to retirement, the more grayness in their hearts, the less life appeals to them. The only antidote for lifelessness is life. What is essential now is that we do something that is valued for itself.

Only one thing is necessary now: we must choose to begin a new kind of life, related to the past, of course, but free of strictures that bind us to it. We must see what we do in it as good. We must find it life-giving ourselves. We must be a gift to the world some way, somehow, for someone.

It's those who go into this period of life washed out, dried up, angry, hurt, humiliated, and resisting for whom newness is a bane rather than a blessing. These people sit sullen or listless in a chair, not reviving themselves, not vivifying anyone else in life, either. They bring no joy to the world because they have no joy to give. They become grumpy old men, whining old women—*not* because that is what old age is about, but because they have chosen to be less than what they are meant to be. They have chosen to be less than what God has in mind for them these years—another kind of fullness of life, another kind of usefulness.

We don't change as we get older—we just get to be more of what we've always been. There is the temptation to let our guard down as we get older, as if we were entitled now to be less than the best of ourselves. We are tempted to expose the unfinished parts of ourselves and do nothing to finish them.

But we are here to depart from this world as finished as we can possibly become. Old age is not when we stop growing. It is exactly the time to grow in new ways. It is the period in which we set out to make sense out of all the growing we have already done. It is the softening season when everything in us is meant to achieve its sweetest, richest, most unique self.

This is the season for sitting back and asking ourselves what the various moments of our lives—both great and small—have been about in the grand scheme. Did our lives have a consistency to them? Did they make sense? Did they have a center and a purpose and a direction and a spiritual identity? And if so—or if not—what is the conclusion of that reckoning to which we must give total attention now? Who are we, after all this time, all this making of a life?

It's frightening, this newness. We hardly know ourselves— our real selves—anymore. We have spent so many years doing what was expected of us, or on the contrary, refusing to do what was expected of us, that discovering this person called the self may be as much a mystery to ourselves as it must be to those around us.

Now we have to ask ourselves, have we ever said what we

really thought to anyone? Have we ever done what we really wanted to do? And what has that done to us—both good and bad? Most of all, what is that telling us about here and now?

We have to want the newness of older age in order to make it the energizing period it has the power to be. It is not a period without purpose. It is not a time of rampant narcissism. It is the point of life in which everything we have learned up until this point can now be put to use.

We have not come to this period for ourselves only.

This period is a new period of spiritual development that is meant to be more than the development of the self. Otherwise how to explain all this experience, all this insight we bring to it? It is about something, for our own sake, and for the sake of the entire human community. It cannot be nothingness for the sake of nothingness.

A burden of these years is the feeling of finality that comes from knowing that this time, however much of it is left, is the end time. Then the weight of what is left to be finished in us takes its toll.

A blessing of these years is that we can, if we will, make them something glorious, a kind of shooting star across the sky of the human race.

ACCOMPLISHMENT

"No one was ever so completely skilled in the conduct of life," Jonathan Swift said, "as not to receive new information from age and experience."

What is the major difference between us and other countries around the world? There are multiple ways to answer the question, of course, but there is one indicator of social difference that may be even more telling than the standard political or economic indices—and that is the age level of the population. In the United States now, the median age of the population is thirty-six. In many parts of the world, it is twenty-five—or younger.

The United States, in other words, is a graying population.

But not graying only. We are also thriving. By the year 2030, for the first time in history, the number of those under seventeen and those over sixty-five will be almost equal. Children are living through infancy and adults are living well into old age. In 1900, forty percent of the population was under seventeen, and only four percent was over sixty-five.[11] Not now. Not here.

Over ten percent of the population—thirty-three million Americans—is now sixty-five and older. By 2030 that number is expected to have more than doubled, to nearly seventy million.[12]

That is important in a lot of ways, of course. It explains the changing demands for hospitals, for senior-citizen complexes, and for intergenerational communities. It also signals the growing political power of a generation that soon will make up twenty-five percent of the voting-age population of the entire country.[13] It will affect what companies produce in years to come and to what portion of the society they will appeal. We can already see the shift in TV commercials from the emphasis on sports equipment twenty-five years ago to health food products now. We're even advertising our funeral plans now in order "not to burden our children"—most of whom may well not even be living near us as we age.

Diminishment is no longer the principal characteristic of aging. On the contrary, we are now developing in ways that only a short time ago would have been considered impossible for anyone over the age of forty.

Old age is no longer a custodial care proposition. Grandma does not "live in" anymore. She is far more likely to live alone, in her own home or apartment, drive a car into her eighties, and volunteer at the local library.

Diminishment is not what we're about—either in terms of numbers or of age.

We eat better, live with less chance of physical disability, have sight and hearing aids, and participate in all levels of society for years. Not only are we the healthiest population of oldsters modern history has known, but we are the most active as well. And these trends are not just found in the industrial nations.

As standards of living increase everywhere, so does the aging population of each region.

But longevity is not the only indicator of the essential changes of age. Now we know that the brain, too—once thought to be irretrievably doomed to progressive senility as the years went by—continues to develop in new ways. It not only goes on producing new cells, but it also develops new ways of thinking.

Scientists have discovered that older people, while not as quick computationally as younger people, do think just as well as the young, but differently—with more depth, with more reflection, with more philosophical awareness. Thought processes of the young compared with the thought processes of the older become the difference between the quickness of a computer game and the quality of a logician. The young produce ideas in rapid quantity, but often without form or figure. Older people might reflect on the very same data younger people do, but instead of manipulating it, tend to reduce it to concepts.

These findings may confound younger generations who have been taught to fear their own old age, but they place a new kind of responsibility, a new way of looking at the world on older people, too. There is no excuse now for simply dropping out of life. As long as we breathe we have a responsibility for the cocreation of the world, for the good of the human race.

Old age is not a free ride to irresponsibility. Now we must take our place among the sages of the world, comparing, evaluating, cajoling, and bringing experience to bear as have the elders of every generation before us.

Now, too, we have a responsibility to mentor the generations after us in the values and ideals that built a society based on equality, respect for others, and pluralism. More than that, we have the spiritual responsibility to see life as a moral force rather than simply a private enterprise.

We need to come to understand to the center of our souls that age is not a disease. It is a new experience in how to live life, how to milk it dry of goodness, of energy, of gratitude, of calm and quiet creativity.

The burden of a lack of commitment to accomplishment means that we have moved into a period of suspended animation, that aging is nothing more than deterioration. The truth is that aging means aging. Nothing more, nothing less. It is just us grown ripe.

The blessing of a commitment to accomplishment is that, as we continue to bring our considerable skills, experience, and insight to bear on the present needs of humankind, we will certainly become wiser, definitely spiritually stronger, and more than ever a blessing to the rest of society.

POSSIBILITY

"We turn not older with years, but newer every day," Emily Dickinson wrote.

Why? Because life begins new again every day—and we must be up to it. Then, unless we foreclose on life ourselves, unless we refuse to live to the hilt every day, we are new again, too.

"I never thought I'd get to be this old," the woman said. "Isn't it wonderful?" She was quick-witted and spry. The latest bout with a worn-out hip didn't seem to faze her at all. Her daughters had brought the walker with them, just in case, but she waved it away when she walked in and crossed the room herself. She was very close to being ninety. The smile said sixty-five, the quick answers said maybe seventy. Nothing about her fit the hackneyed expectations of what it is to be ninety.

When someone in the group offered to go to the buffet table for her, she shot back, "Why? I can get them for myself." Then she said with the glee of the newly invincible, "Look . . . no hands." And she got out of the heavy overstuffed recliner as easily as anyone else in the room.

Here was a woman whose husband had been long dead, whose daughters were in their sixties themselves, whose sons lived states away, who had given up her own home years ago and had been going from one apartment to another for years now. She was happy, and funny, and very, very alive.

She was, in fact, more typical of the new elderly than we often enough stop to realize.

Our image of an aging population is more commonly an image of debilitation and dependence, of unhappy isolation and social uselessness, of sad souls exiled to the fringes of life and left living alone in a world long gone.

But people live longer every decade that passes. And they live alone. And they have, gerontological data now tells us, very few years of helplessness. Aging, at least in the developed world, is instead a period of sweet liberation and possibility.

Yet it is also commonly a period of great dislocation. The modern world may be full of "retirement plans," but who can really plan much? And be sure of it? Life is not a straight line, we learn. It is, if anything, a spiral.

Older people move out of neighborhoods where they have lived countless years. They move into small apartments surrounded by people they have never met before. They give up social networks and old haunts, beloved pets and positions of status and prestige, steady jobs and salary raises in a society in which the median income of women and men over sixty-five is between $12,000 and $20,000 a year.[14]

In fact, discontinuity may be one of the defining factors of age in the modern world.

But this dislocation and discontinuity is also something else. It is the moment of late but emancipating possibility.

Who hasn't gone through a period in life when they wished they could simply disappear and start all over again? What most of us do not realize is that today old age *is* that new life. And we must all deal with it, in one way or the other. The gift is recognizing the potential of it, both spiritual and social, and knowing what to do with it.

We get to make new friends, to develop new activities, new routines, new social circles with them. We begin to do untried things in unprecedented places. And we get to tell all the old stories to a whole new group of people.

There is a startling experience of variety in it all. A kind of giddy sense of possibility.

We no longer have to wear the old roles that so defined us for so many years. We can be funny and silly and irresponsible for a change. We can buy new things without asking someone for permission to get them.

We can even begin to think differently now. And we do!

An inner authority seems to emerge out of nowhere. We question things we never even thought of thinking about before, let alone doubt them. And now that we're no longer the enforcers of the family we can enjoy younger people a great deal more than we ever did before, judge them less, welcome them always with an open heart.

We sit and listen to them talk to us because they trust our trust in them, our mercy, our freedom of heart. Things change, we know now. We're sure of that, because we have changed. For the first time in our lives, we start to take people for who they are—now and here—because who knows better than we do that we all transform before we die.

We are unloosed, in some ways for the first time ever. And, if we are really healthy personalities, we find ourselves intent on living this new stage of life to the end, squeezing out of it every grace, every delight, every exciting new idea, every intriguing answer to every plaguing question.

All of that takes energy, of course, and just at the moment in life when we might think we don't have any energy left. Everything has seemed so tiring for so long, we would hardly recognize ourselves if we weren't so tired. But tiredness is what creates tiredness. The only way to get over being tired is to do something. Invite someone to go to a show, for instance. Learn to golf, join a social club, go to the pool at the Y, plan a vacation to the big city or a national park. Begin a whole new routine with another cluster of friends—and build another life together.

A burden of these years is to assume that when the great change from being defined and delimited by the past—however good it may have been—is over, that life is over.

A blessing of these years is to realize, early, that this stage of life is full of possibilities, full of the desire to go on living, to seize the independence, to create new activities and networks of interesting new people.

ADJUSTMENT

"To know how to grow old," the Swiss philosopher Henri Frédéric Amiel wrote, "is the master work of wisdom and one of the most difficult chapters in the great art of living."

The life changes that come so commonly with the later years of life require untried ways of going about the exercise of living. Hardest of all, they come whether we want them to or not. We find ourselves in strange circumstances with late-found friends after a lifetime of old relationships disappear or new conditions engulf us. Then it is not nearly so much what happens to us as the way we choose to deal with what happens to us. It is not an easy time.

Indeed, this is the last great period of human growth for us. It is the scaling of the final mountains of adjustment, of newness, of change, of spiritual development. It demands of us every bit of strength, every ounce of belief in the holiness of the universe that we have left to give.

For those who have the luxury of aging at home—the house I have lived in all my adult life, the city he grew up in, the neighborhood she loves—aging is almost always simply the continuation

of life as it has been before. Aging then is simply another phase of
the same. After all, I have been here in this place for many years.
I know the people and the stores, the buses and the whole town.
I am still part of it. It is all simply an extension of me. Everything
is familiar. Everything is safe. However many years I've accumulated, in fact, they are almost irrelevant in situations like this. I am
still, I feel, what I have always been. My professional world may
have disappeared, yes, but not my life.

There are changes even here, of course, but small ones. I
begin to do a little less. I don't go out to work every morning.
I'm not as inclined to drive at night. I don't have the number
of dinner parties I once had. But, other than that, there are
few discernible differences between being sixty-four and sixty-
seven, between being sixty-nine or seventy-four. Life lived like
this remains basically the same, however many the seasons.

Clearly, the first great confrontation with age comes with
separation from the familiar. When the world that was and the
world that is are on opposite sides of a fault line, the present
unlike what was before, when the lifelines shatter, then real
change has arrived. Then age comes roaring into consciousness
with a whole new timbre. Then the idea of aging and becoming
"old" sharpens in focus for me. My soul begins to change hue.
I find myself struggling to stay psychologically alive, however
strong my body seems to be.

First the job goes, then the house goes, then the precious
things begin to go, one little piece at a time to the children,
one old box after another to the thrift shop folks. Then the
privacy goes, then the dog and the cat, the desk and the papers,
the trips and eventually the car. Then, finally, for the first time,
the self goes.

The person I once knew myself to be—friendly, happy, easy-going, satisfied—stands in danger of going, too. The old edge to the old temper becomes more difficult to control. Interest in other people begins to wane in favor of sitting, lights out, in the twilight, living with my losses. The frown becomes permanent. The smile turns terse.

All the danger signals are there to see. Someone young—me—is dying, years before my time. And the only person who can save me from myself is myself. Then I begin to understand as never before that holiness is made of dailiness, of living life as it comes to me, not as I insist it be.

It's time to reach down into the center of the soul and consider what is happening to me. It isn't that the changes aren't difficult. Of course they are. It's only that, for my own sake, difficult as they may be, I cannot allow them to become terminal. Life goes on—and I must, too. But how?

How can we possibly defend ourselves from a situation such as this? How do we deal with things we do not want to deal with, however good they may in themselves be? How do we cope with what we feel we cannot endure? And the simple, but troubling, answer is that there is no such thing as not coping. Cope we will, if for no other reason than that we have to. The only issue is whether we will choose to cope well—or poorly.

Learning how to cope with the vagaries of life is a long-term project. We begin early in life to experiment—we blame others for whatever situation we're in, for instance, or we sulk to let the world know we don't like it. Then, eventually, we learn that pouting and blaming solve nothing and, instead, only add to the pain we're feeling.

The truth is that there are no circumstances in life more

important than being able to deal well with the changes that come as we age. These are the coping skills that will take us to the end. The happiness of the last years of our life depends on them.

All coping skills are not the same, however. Psychology defines the differences between them for us.[15] There are, on the lowest level, coping mechanisms that simply enable us to opt out of the situation entirely. Some people, under the stress of change, become delusional, for instance. They break with reality completely. They go into what the medical community calls "premature senility." They let go of their grasp on life. They slip. They become withdrawn or even incoherent. We know they have lost touch with life, like a person at sea who simply lets go of the rope connected to the boat.

But these are the rare cases. More than likely, we stay very much alert to what is happening. We engage with it. We talk about it. We even obsess over it. In the end, we have two choices. We find ourselves faced with social options that will either serve to make the new life an energizing and exciting experience—or we resist the change to the point that we become resistance itself.

This resistance is the next level of coping. These people are functional but painfully immature in their emotional reactions. Yes, they go through the routines of life. They continue to do the wash, or take their medicine, or keep up some kind of personal appearances. But, at the same time, they are not the persons we know them to be. Their souls spoil in their shells. Little by little, in small, clear ways, they begin to punish the world around them for the situation they're in. When the time finally comes for them to move, they might refuse to pack up to leave the house, or they get sick, or they won't get dressed.

The message is clear: if you want me to be ready to leave here, you will have to do it yourself. Or they begin the blame game: other people are responsible for this, not me, not my condition, not my finances. But definitely not I. "If my doctor had treated me earlier for this, I wouldn't have to leave here," they say. Or, "It's my daughter's fault I can't live alone. She could cook for me if she wanted to."

This kind of passive aggression and the projection of blame for my situation onto others corrodes what had been good relationships with the people around me, just when I needed them most. What had once been a good personality, balanced and pleasant, is now skewed, distorted, blighted. I become a pouter, a complainer, a weaver of wild dreams no longer possible for someone either my age or in my situation. "Whatever happened to him?" people say. "He was always such a pleasant, easygoing person." And they start to avoid us.

At the third level of coping skills, people may leave a place they've lived in for years with a minimum degree of eruption, but they adapt poorly to their new environment. They don't say much about the move. Instead, they suppress their feelings to the point that they become cold and unresponsive. They turn their anger at being displaced onto the people who manage the new facility they're in, for instance. Nothing is right. Everything—the food, the noise, the care, the cleaning—is below standard. They are, they claim, being ignored or abused or discriminated against. They hide inside their living quarters and refuse to adjust. They simply decline to accept the present situation and keep demanding that people enable them to go back to life as it was before. They get stuck. They stagnate. They grumble. They refuse to move on. Then their families lose them long before they die. It is a long, sad journey for everyone involved. What could be pleasant, livable, freeing becomes a prison for the soul, the gilded cage of the mind. The spirit turns to dust and ash.

But there is another way to deal with these years. Those whose coping mechanisms are mature, those who have spent their lives learning to respond to the difficulties of life with aplomb and courage, defend themselves from the stress of major change by making light of it. They feel the pain of it, but they turn the pain into some kind of new gift.

"See my new mansion," the old woman said as she showed off the tiny one-room efficiency apartment she'd moved into after they sold her home. "I should have had everything on one floor when I had all the children. This lovely place is years too late," she laughed. Another woman finally moved into the local retirement living center, without a word. She never went back to her house, though there were many who would have gladly taken her there at any time. "No, love," she said to a young friend, "I don't have to go back. This is my home now." And she waved her hand toward the large visiting parlor in the front of the building. "There are so many people here who need help. There is so much for me to do here."

Clearly, such individuals have attained spiritual adulthood. They handle pain by replacing it with new joys. They begin to attend to the struggles of others in order to transcend their own. They live in anticipation of life's elemental joys—fresh flowers on the table, the small balcony overlooking the communal garden, the chance to make new friends in the building, the opportunity to go about life without worrying about the roof or the yard or the housecleaning. They simply refuse to allow themselves to live in the past, to live in the gloom of their memories. "Time marches on," they say, and, with a smile for everyone they meet, they march with it.

They are a sign to a younger generation that yes, there is life after seventy. Lots of it. If only we'll make it for ourselves.

A burden of these years is that we must consciously decide how we will live, what kind of person we will become now, what kind of personality and spirituality we will bring into every group, how alive we intend to be.

A blessing of these years is being able to live so open-heartedly, and to adjust so well, that others can look to us and see what being old can bring in terms of life, of holiness, of goodness to make the world new again.

FULFILLMENT

In Plato's view, "Old age has a great sense of calm and freedom when the passions have relaxed their hold and have escaped not from one master but from many."

Youth is a cauldron of hot issues—career and excitement, dating and mating, succeeding and failing.

Middle age is the culmination of those events. Now we are immersed in bringing the decisions we made in younger days to some kind of completion. We want to be recognized in our work. We need to raise children of our own. We are busy getting "established"—in the civic community, in the business, in the family, in the social life of the town. We are busy, busy, busy every moment. We run and we work and we work and we run. Life is one long emotional revolving door. It carries us from one high to another, through one low to the next. In middle age life is often lived on the brink.

But then somewhere in the midst of the emotional throes of middle age, we settle in. We learn that most crises are not really crises at all. They are simply life. Then somewhere along the way, we stop being so intent about it. We begin to find a balance.

By the time aging strikes its chord in our hearts, we have been prepared to meet it, even-handedly, resolutely, cheerfully. Then we are at last able to look life in the eye and stare it down.

The women and men Plato talks about—serene and satisfied, comfortable with themselves and happy with what they have, proud of what they've done and completely at ease with the fact that they aren't doing it anymore—are everywhere. We have all seen them, been struck by the ease with which they go through life. We don't talk about them much, though. After all, what would happen to this hard-driving, blood-letting economy of ours if the rest of society ever realized how many of them there are. All doing well. All living a life beyond the long commute and the evening traffic jams. And all of them not interested in what it would mean to grasp for more.

Doris had been a college professor for years. Climbing the academic ladder as a woman in an era of women's rights brought a kind of high to life she never thought could ever be possible. There were promotions and tenure and department positions in the making. There was even some talk of her moving to a more prestigious university that was now head-hunting women in order to claim its credentials as an equal employment institution. But no. She liked the small town and the volunteer work she did there with children's theater. So, after retirement, she stayed in the little old house in the center of the city and did puppet shows with street children.

Bill was a therapist who worked twelve hours a day. Person after person after person, made unhealthy by the hectic lives they were living, came to him for help to find some kind of balance, to calm down a bit, to find the courage it takes to start over. And he never said no. Eventually, however, the strain of listening to them for hours on end began to affect his own sense of well-being. He closed the practice and moved out of state to give them all an example of another way of living. Today, he manages a property or two and gives money to charities that work with those who have no money at all.

Such are the spiritual refugees from this land called the global economy, big business, corporate greed, insatiability. And how do we account for them in a society that gears people to identify more with power and social status than it does with living life itself? How is it that some of us seek the retirement that others just as desperately resist?

Only age teaches us that there is such a thing as reaching so high that our projects succeed, but our life quality declines. Lives that seem to have succeeded are often shattered by these very successes.

Age is the antidote to personal destruction, the call to spiritual growth, because age finally brings us to the point where there is nowhere else to go but inside for comfort, inside for wealth, inside for the things that really count.

It is the damping-down time of life. Our passions and flaws—anger, jealousy, envy, pride—subside to the point that we begin to awaken to another whole level of life. The interior life, the search for the sacred, takes over to the point that we can begin to assess how much energy the passions and flaws have drained from our life.

Pride has led us to strive for things so far above us we have forgotten who we really are.

Old angers have simmered in us for so many years we have

blocked good times with invisible bile. Now they finally begin to fade. What is it that we were so exercised about anyway? And was it worth all that spleen?

Envy has led us astray far too many times. What we wanted, we discover when we finally get it, doesn't really change much at all. We are still who we always were, restless and without direction.

Lust sapped us of the energy it takes to make relationships last. We focused on the thrill of the chase rather than on the meaning of the relationship. And we got stung so many times.

Gluttony left us always hungry for more of everything. We lost the capacity to be satisfied and wasted a part of life gorging ourselves on what does not last.

Sloth entombed us in ourselves. We waited for life to come to us and failed, as a result, to discipline ourselves to do what was good for us ourselves.

Covetousness led us to miss the qualities in ourselves in order to concentrate on the things around us. We have wanted what other people had to the point that we failed to appreciate the blessings of our own lives.

But as we get older the gleam goes off the gold. There is a point at which money can do absolutely nothing for us but buy us more and more expensive toys with which to try to fill up our spiritual emptiness.

When we have consumed ourselves with the fire of ambition, destroyed ourselves with the desire for power, then there is nothing left for us but to take refuge in whatever warm coals of the soul we have managed to maintain, even if we failed to fan them.

Now the passions quiet and these old coals of wonder and

insight and soul-centeredness come alive in us. Surprisingly, we come to understand that whatever we have is enough. And life itself becomes rich again. Nothing eats away at us now. Nothing drives us beyond our grasp anymore. Nothing is left to us now but our selves. And, we come to realize, it is enough.

We are no longer at the mercy of the self. It is time to taste the essence of life rather than concern ourselves with its accessories. It has taken almost a lifetime to love a sunset, to value company, to give up what has always been too much, and to learn to revel in what is enough—but it has been worth the wait.

A burden of these years is the awareness of all that we missed for so long while we sold our souls to the idols of the time.

A blessing of these years is the equanimity that comes from knowing that none of the side roads of life were really wasted. Truth is, we learned something invaluable on each of them. We learned that to come to fullness of life it takes absolutely nothing at all beyond the development of the best in ourselves.

MYSTERY

"For age is opportunity no less / Than youth itself, though in another dress," Henry Wadsworth Longfellow observed. "And as the evening twilight fades away / The sky is filled with stars, invisible by day."

Longfellow speaks clearly of the mystery of the later years of life, the satisfaction of it all. And yet one of the obstacles to living an exciting life in our later years is that we become so sure we're losing something and so unaware of what we're gaining.

So much in life is aimed at either youth or middle age. Almost nothing points us to the days when time alone will be our guide, our companion, our goal. We have few or no promises about the glories of being less busy, less harried, less consumed by everything. The later years of life are given to us to bring in the harvest of all that effort.

But to live into the mystery of this stage of life, it is important to allow ourselves to break out of the confines of the old one with all its social rigors and personal needs and public roles and protocols. We have learned so well how to live the rules of life. We are not so sure how to live its freedoms.

The sad thing about modern living is that we so easily and quickly become cemented in our personal little worlds. For years, we walk the same streets, follow the same schedules, eat the same food, talk to the same people, read the same papers, have the same conversations over and over again.

The problem is that there is simply no time to stroll down strange streets or waste precious moments in the exploration of small boutiques. If we're not home by seven every night, we can't get the laundry done. A shopping list is faster than browsing in those dusty old markets or exploring gourmet food stores where they sell seven types of plain yogurt and seventy kinds of cheese. There is simply no way to meet new people when office parties and business meetings all take place at the same restaurant over and over again. We have no way to talk to new people on a long commute and, besides, there is not much left to say when politics, economics, and religion are all off the superficial civil list.

Eventually routine seeps into every dimension of life. Some of it is comforting, of course. Routine is what lets us know what to do and just when and how to do it. But much of it is stultifying. It turns us into lower-level robots who do not think enough to realize that we're not thinking much about anything at all.

It's that from which old age liberates us. Routine can finally give way to mystery, to possibility, to the grazing time of life.

The problem is that it can take a long, long time before it feels like a liberation. We resist it mightily. We make our own prisons and live in them till we're too numb to try to get away.

Only getting older frees us, despite ourselves, from ourselves.

Being older is what gives us the opportunity to stray as we have never strayed in our lives. We could go to the cabin on Wednesday, for instance. Well, why not? We could go down to the library and sit in the reading room and read all day. Well, why not? We could play cards with a sick neighbor today. Well, why not? We can sit in the car at the edge of the water and read a book. Well, why not? Why not, in fact, walk into the mystery of life until we are comfortable enough with mystery to trust it even at the end?

Schedules and deadlines have a place in life, of course. They keep us accountable to society. The problem starts when they rule our lives, when they obstruct our lives, when they become our lives.

Mystery is what happens to us when we allow life to evolve rather than having to make it happen all the time. It is the strange knock at the door, the sudden sight of an unceremoniously blooming flower, an afternoon in the yard, a day of riding the midtown bus. Just to see. Just to notice. Just to be there.

There is something holy-making about simply presuming that what happens to us in any given day is sent to awaken our souls to something new: another smell, a different taste, a moment when we allow ourselves to lock eyes with a stranger, to smile a bit, to nod our head in greeting. Who knows? Maybe one of those things will open us to the refreshing memory of pain, a poignant reminder of glory, a breathless moment of astonishment, a sense of the presence of God in life.

The sunlight brings back in new shades of color the meaning of a moment long ago. Astonishment shakes us into conscious awareness of things long seen, but long unseen as well. Those things are of the essence of mystery.

There is purpose to mystery in a coolly calculated world. We live lives that are so precisely timed now. Before people owned watches, dawn and dark were enough of a frame to live by. "I'll come tomorrow" meant I will be there when I get there tomorrow. Now, "I'll come tomorrow" only means when, precisely: by the minute, to the moment. No mystery there. Just expectation.

So mystery, the notion that something wonderful can happen at any time if we will only allow space for it, takes us into a whole new awareness of the immanence of God in time. God comes, we learn now, when we least expect it. Maybe most likely of all when we least expect it.

For the most part, we have learned to deny the right of the unexpected, the mysterious, to invade our neatly scheduled lives at all. Too risky that, in a world that lives precariously balanced on tight schedules and in the light of menacing deadlines.

But oh, in age, mystery comes alive. Nothing is very sure anymore. Everything speaks of maybe and perhaps, might and possibly. I might still be here. And I might not. Like children, we learn to wonder again. We learn that getting up every day can be fun, can be wonder-full. Something will surely happen. What will it be?

Then, as the years go by, we learn to trust the goodness of time, the glorious cornucopia of life called God. And who knows? At the end of life, the mystery waiting for us there, finally visible under the glare of time, may be more than the soul can hold.

A burden of these years is to fear the ever-approaching mystical before us, as if the God-ness we have known in life will desert us in death.

A blessing of these years is coming to see that behind everything so stolid, so firm, so familiar in front of us runs a descant of mystery and meaning to be experienced in ways we never thought possible before. To become free of the prosaic and the scheduled and the pragmatic is to break the world open in ways we never dreamed of. In this new world, a mountain, a bench, a grassy path is far more than simply itself. It is a symbol of unprecedented possibilities, of the holiness of time.

RELATIONSHIPS

"Old age is an island surrounded by death," wrote the Ecuadorian essayist Juan Montalvo.

At its core, life is not about things, it is about relationships. It is the hands we go on holding in our hearts at the end that define the kind of life we have led. Our relationships determine the quality of life as we have known it. They show us the face of God on Earth. They are, too, what batter our hearts into the feelings of life.

When the relationships we forge as we go begin to disappear, our own life changes. We know then what it is to be abandoned, to be a little less impervious to feeling than we thought we were. Now it is not things we need, it is understanding we crave. It is understanding that draws us out of ourselves into the earthenware vessel of new life.

We watch the ones we love leave us, and we find ourselves at another crossover moment in time. What do we do now? Go on alone? Stop and withdraw into ourselves? Risk the chance of becoming a friend again? It is a life-changing question. It is a soul-changing answer. And, for fear we might miss the lesson of it, the pain of it is everywhere.

On this particular Sunday, traffic was thin and the dock was quiet. Nothing seemed to block the flow of cars around the dock—but nothing was moving, either. In the middle of the dock lay a dead duck, her soft feathers hanging limp along the ground. But that was not the story. The story was about loss. Around the duck at a respectful distance, quiet, heads down, necks curved silently over the water, were a great many other ducks. Some of them were swaying silently in the moving waters of the bay. Others of them had landed on the dock itself, circled the dead one and lowed over it, like mourners in a Grecian drama. And there in the middle, circling the dead creature wildly, wings flapping, head thrown back, screaming and screeching in pain was a lone mallard, inconsolable, howling for help. "Ducks are monogamous," a man said to no one in particular as he walked away. "They mate for life."

For anyone who has ever watched a friend go through the very same thing, the meaning is clear: once our mates go, so, in a way, do we.

When that happens, two temptations eat at the cloth of old age. The first is the temptation to live in a world long gone, to condemn ourselves to existing almost exclusively among a collection of graying photographs. The second is the attempt to insulate ourselves from life by avoiding the risk of further vulnerability, by allowing emotional death to take us before physical death arrives.

For a long time, in fact, people laughed scornful, sneering laughs at old people who fell in love. Marriage was out of the question. Sexuality, let alone sexual expression, was not a given.

A world built on youthful sex, on the procreative dimensions of marriage, saw something obscene about the whole notion of intense sexual and loving relationships among older people. The primary purpose of marriage had for so long been defined as child-rearing that the role of adult relationships, especially in later life, had been dismissed.

Procreation—not companionship, not friendship, not love—had been the main object of marriage for centuries. Women were bought and sold, "given" in marriage to whatever relationships seemed politically, economically advantageous to the families involved, whatever the effect on the couple itself. Heirs were the goal, rulers and field workers and human old-age security systems. Thus, the need for intimacy, for support, for mutual care went the way of age. Love was physical and so ended with the ebbing of its physical functions. After that, apparently, people were expected to go through life aloof and emotionally alone.

As a result, unlike those in any other phase of life, older people are forced to deal with the challenge of two very different types of relationships.

First, they have to deal with the haunting presence of relationships they have lost to death or distance. For all of us, the dying take a part of us into the grave with them—like conversations that can never be completed, dreams that can never be fulfilled. But for the elderly, the death of spouses, of loved ones, of friends, takes even more away—the memories, the sense of self, the feeling of community. If truth were known, too often the dead take the energy of the living, too.

When the funeral of a dear friend is over, we know with a new kind of pain that another road has closed for us. There is one less friend to walk with now, and the list is getting shorter every day. When a spouse dies, the insatiable emptiness is even worse. Who cares for us now? Who really wants us here? Without doubt, the life of the one left behind has been indelibly changed—has, it seems, ended.

Second, older people struggle with the effort it takes to make new friends, new companions, in their own world, which is becoming ever more removed from the faster-moving world around them. "Retirement villages," high on amenities but often low on mixed populations, are springing up everywhere. Hotel chains are focusing now on the development of managed-retirement communities where an older generation will live in small independent apartments, at least until after the age of eighty-five.[16]

True, most seniors are healthy, alert, and totally functional. But it requires effort and energy to make new friends now. And is it even worth the time? Friendship, after all, let alone love, takes a great deal of tending, a lot of talking, more getting-to-know-you time than we ourselves may have left. So why bother?

The temptation to disengage is severe. And yet, our need for understanding, for comfort, for the sense of presence that comes with the voice at the other end of a phone call is greater than ever.

How is this shell of a life ever to be filled again? And if it is not filled, is there any real life yet to be had?

The fact is that relationships are the alchemy of life. They turn the dross of dailiness into gold. They make human community real. They provide what we need and wait in turn for us to give back. They are a sign of the presence of a loving God in life. There is no such thing at any stage of human development as life without relationships. In this later stage then, the only uncertainty is whether we will decide to live inside ourselves, alone with our past relationships, or trust that the life made glorious by others in the past can be made glorious again—by new meetings, new moments, new spirit.

For that to happen, we ourselves need to reach out first. We need to make ourselves interesting again. We need to learn again how to invite people into our lives—in to watch the game or play cards together, in to eat or read books together. Then, we need to make the effort to go out to places where people our own age gather, as well as to events where the generations mix and the fun comes from meeting new people and talking about different things.

> *A burden of these years is that being alone, bad as it feels, is easier than doing what it takes to be with someone else. It would be so much easier now simply to close the sunshades of our soul and give up. So much easier simply to wait for death to claim what has already died in us—a love for life and a trust in its essential goodness. So we cut ourselves out of our own lives and watch them wither away.*

> *A blessing of these years is that they offer us the chance to be excited by new personalities, new warmth, new activities, new people all over again. Does it demand that we fall in love? No. But it does demand that we love someone else enough to be just as interested in them as we are in ourselves. It demands that we set out to make tomorrow happy.*

TALE-TELLING

"For the unlearned," the Hasidim say, "old age is winter; for the learned, it is the season of harvest."

It is the distribution of that harvest to the rest of the human community for which we look to the elders among us. Old age is a treasure-house of history—personal history, family history, national history, world history. But what do we do with everything an older generation knows in a culture that does not seek answers from that generation? Every elder in every community is a living story for the people to whom he or she will someday leave the Earth to guide as good, as better, than they did in their own time.

In the older members of every society lies the taproot of that society. It goes down deeper into the past than any others. The elders know where every idea has come from. And why. They know what it means—what it really means—to be family, to be citizen, to be free, to be enslaved. They know the difference between evolution and revolution. And, most of all, they know that there is room for both in the development of the world in which we live.

But more important even than their knowledge is their ability, their call, to pass those stories on to the later generations. Without the passing on of the stories, the young ones are a group without character, without tradition, without the living memory of how and why they came together in the first place.

Family tales have always been the parables one generation handed down to the next to tell us who we are and where we came from. Funeral rituals, the interment of ancestors, became the art form that preserved the values and ideals of the past in special ways. Meant to remind the clan of their connections in both life and death, funerals were a tribal event. Telling the stories of those who passed away made family the bridge to both past and future.

Even in our own times, in the not so distant past, the deceased were laid out in the family homes. But while it was prayer time for the soul of the dead in the parlor, in the rest of the house it was story-telling time for the living.

These were the moments when families told themselves who they were and who they had wanted to be. In those moments children learned the history of their parents' own childhood. Most of all, the young came to realize what stood to be lost forever in one last breath if the next generation did not take responsibility for maintaining it.

Family folklore about war and work, about marriage and sickness, about family shame and family glories, about the strength of the family to endure and the dangers of weakness came pouring out, good and bad together. The lessons were immortal ones: God was good and God was a judge. War was horrible or it was glorious. Leaving the family was dangerous or necessary. Money could not be counted on to give us a good life, and, in the end, the only ones who could save us from ourselves were we ourselves.

The tale-telling of the older people became the catechism of the family. These were the life lessons meant to make us all stronger, wiser, and truer.

It is those stories told in front of a fire, in the kitchen during a wake, at parties and memorial services, at holidays that become the fiber of a family, a group, a people. These stories become the living history that binds us together.

But only the old can tell the tales with both conviction and meaning. Only the old bear within their own bodies the truth of each story itself. Only they authenticate our right to live the story, too, in our own times, for the sake of our own children and history and people and nation.

Being tale-bearer is of the essence of growing old. The tale-bearers are proof of the authenticity of the past. They determine what truth will be for all of us. Their stories will carry us all into the days to come. When grandfathers tell stories of the majesties of war and fail to tell of its ghoulishness, its orgies of horror, they plant the seeds of the next glorious lie in the minds of the young ones. When grandmothers tell of the pain of childbirth but not its ecstasy, they make it more difficult to delight in the idea of giving birth. When any of us fail to listen to the stories being handed down to us, we lose the opportunity to hear the life lessons and must then learn the hard way ourselves.

The burden of tale-telling is to think that by avoiding our responsibility to be part of living history we will stay forever young. By not telling those who follow us the stories of what it took to get here, we fail the harvest of our own life and the plowing days of theirs.

The blessing that comes with tale-telling is the awareness that we have now done our duty to life. We have distilled our experiences to the point that they can become useful to someone younger.

LETTING GO

"When physical eyesight declines," Plato said, "spiritual eyesight increases."

It is this spiritual eyesight, the ability to see into the inner meaning of things, the spiritual value of things, the essential core of things, that must carry us from this point on. And it is the spiritual essence of a person that emerges from the natural divestment that comes with old age. Life, it seems, follows a relentless cycle: in our early years we accumulate, but in our later years we divest. Both of them have a place in life. Both of them are a struggle. Both of them are liberating.

In the early years, life is a series of milestones. The first words, the first steps, the first book, the first bike, and the first graduation. Then the grasping begins. We must get an education, get a job, get a life. In this period of life, growing means getting.

Every step along the way is marked again by the things that are the sign of it. Now it is a matter of getting the right credentials—the college degree, the technician's license, the professional certifications, the promotions. And all the while, parents and friends, relatives and mentors worry about us. They worry if we start the climb late, or if we climb too fast or too slowly, too intently or not intently enough. But whatever the pace, the concentration is on the climb.

And we know if we're doing it right because there are markers along the way that measure the success of it all. The job. The bank account. Our own car. And the trips that mark our rites of passage. We backpack across Europe, or go camping in the Grand Canyon, or buy a motorbike and ride through the Rockies, or we go with our buddies to the big city, to celebrate our coming of age. Then, they say, we settle down.

But oh, the journey is far from over. On the contrary. Settling down, we discover, is not settling down at all. It has its own criteria. Its own struggles. Its own trophies to gather. It is one long exercise in accumulation. Now comes the career and the apartment, the titles and the mortgages, the children and their graduations, the social life and the weddings. And, at long last, the retirement party.

Then we have arrived at the great crossover moment in time. The time for heaping up is over. All we know now is that whatever we have managed to accumulate at the end of the climb is just about all we'll ever get. Did we succeed or not?

The grade we now get in "Living" is not given by someone else, as it was in the course of the earlier achievements. This time we have to grade ourselves. The question now is, how and by what measures do we decide if our life has been a success?

And strangely enough, at this time, we find that one of life's major tasks is to determine what to do with everything we have managed to gather so far. Do we give it away to family and friends? Sell it to antique dealers? Pack it up for thrift shops?

Write a journal of the memories that every piece of it replays in us?

All of a sudden, none of the old milestone markers really counts for much. But what does?

When we get to that point, it is clear that the next part of life has finally begun for us.

Every major spiritual tradition knows as one of its core experiences a period of major divestment, of total renunciation of that which shaped a person *before* he or she began the great spiritual quest. In this period, the seeker considers the meaning of life and death, of the spiritual and the material, of Earth and its beyond, of the soul in contact with the great soul within.

This is the period when we evaluate everything we have come to know about life and look for a dimension above the things of this world, for the sake of what is yet to come. The search means, then, that we strip ourselves of whatever it is we have accrued until this time in order to give ourselves wholly to the birthing of the person within. Into this part of life we travel light.

When I look around the crowded room and wonder why I am keeping the large desk when a smaller one would do just as well, something inside of me is beginning to change. When three sets of dishes are two sets too many, I have begun to need more than just things. When the house is too crowded and the car is too big and the perfect lawn too much of a bother, I have begun a whole new adventure in life.

It is the shaping of the soul that occupies us now. Now, consciously or, more likely, not, we set out to find out for ourselves who we really are, what we know, what we care about, and how to be simply enough for ourselves in the world.

Little by little we begin to strip down a layer at a time. We don't run with the business crowd anymore. We discover the neighbor instead.

Then, we leave the old house and the old neighborhood for a smaller place, easier to handle, easier to give up.

We discover what the Kenyans mean when they say, "Those who have cattle have care." And little by little we become less of our outer image and more of our inner selves.

"We come into this world naked and alone," a saying declares, "and we leave it the same way: naked and alone." But not quite. Because by now, we have learned that the things we amassed to prove to ourselves how valuable, how important, how successful we were, didn't prove it at all. In fact, they have very little to do with it all. It's what's inside of us, not what's outside of us that counts. It's what we learned along the way, what we meant to other people along the way, what we became inside—along the way—that is really who we are.

The problem comes for those who are unable to let go. The "relaxed grasp" has never been part of their lives. Somewhere along the line they accepted the heretical notion that what we have is what we are. So, leaving the home leaves them empty and in agony. Giving away the things that marked all the stages of their lives leaves them feeling bereft of themselves. They have not looked inside for so long, they cannot now appreciate that they finally have the time—and the freedom—to furnish the soul with poetry and beauty, with friendships and adventure, with children to play with rather than raise, and with peers to talk to about important matters rather than superficial things.

The time is here. We have a chance to become what all the living has enabled us to be. Now we can make sense of it. But only if we can let go of the past. Only if we can let go of all the old ideas of success, all the old marks of humanity and finally, now, allow ourselves to become simply human instead.

A burden of these years is the temptation to cling to the times and things behind us rather than move to the liberating moments ahead.

A blessing of these years is the invitation to go lightfooted into the here and now—because we spend far too much of life preparing for the future rather than enjoying the present.

LEARNING

"I have enjoyed greatly the second blooming," wrote Agatha Christie, "that comes when you finish the life of the emotions and of personal relations and suddenly find—at the age of fifty, say—that a whole new life has opened before you, filled with things you can think about, study or read about. . . . It is as if a fresh sap of ideas and thoughts was rising in you."

Agatha Christie, still writing bestsellers in her eighties, shattered the very idea of a sclerotic old age. If anything, she is an icon of the link between education and experience, of the notion that learning is not only a lifelong task but also a lifelong summons to renewal of the soul.

The danger in our earlier years is the notion that having completed high school or earned a college degree, we have completed our preparation for life. The problem with degrees is that they wear out quickly or prepare us for only one small area of life, at best. We are still young when the certificates turn yellow on the wall and the knowledge they proclaim is obsolete.

The danger in later years is the myth that older people

cannot learn now as they have in younger years. Fear of mental collapse becomes the anxiety of the age. Perhaps the most common concern mentioned as people approach retirement age is, "I think I must be losing it. . . ." They say it with a laugh—at least at first—but soon it becomes a mantra, if not a silent, gnawing fear. "I can't find my keys again," they say. "How could I forget his name? I worked with him for years," they worry. "I used to know those dates off by heart. Now they're gone; simply gone," they lament. The effects are somewhere between panic and despair. Has it finally happened? Is this what they mean by dementia? The bad news is, maybe. The good news is, probably not. Very unlikely. Not normally.

One of the most positive results of the rising incidence of Alzheimer's disease in a large and aging population is the amount of research now being done on the human brain. Up until this period, the unchallenged assumption was simply that brains age as bodies do, and just as the body declines so does the brain. The common medical conception up to this time was that brains began to shrink at the age of twenty and by the age of seventy would be at least ten percent smaller. By the age of eighty we could simply expect to be totally dysfunctional.[17] The image of the shrinking, atrophic brain loomed large in our minds. Age meant mental deterioration, as surely as the night follows the day. But is that assumption true? No.

Neurological research now confirms that old brains are indeed physically smaller, but no less intellectually competent than young ones. And in some ways, in terms of reflection and creativity, they are even better, if for no other reason than that they have a lot of experience to add to intellectual acuity.

We know now that anomia, the inability to remember names,

is common to anyone over thirty. Likewise with names, and jokes, and spatial cues, and phone numbers. It seems that as the brain ages it begins to sort and discard information that is "emotionally neutral." What doesn't have personal meaning becomes less and less important to us as the years go by, less and less accessible, while matters of emotional impact on the other hand become even fresher. Other mental abilities begin to sharpen as well. We become more reflective, more analytical. We become more able to assimilate and assess data. We begin to notice other dimensions of the world, of people, of events, of ideas beyond data, and to absorb them into our answers. We bring experience to knowledge and then add wisdom to our results.[18]

But only if we continue to develop, to learn, to cultivate our mental acuity as we age.

As Agatha Christie put it, we "bloom" as we grow. New abilities emerge. New insights arise. New vision is possible.

The danger lies in not feeding this growth. The idle mind, the mind left to atrophy, is at risk. With nothing to think about, with no challenges to engage us, with no problems to solve, the question is looming: What is left of me? Why bother? Why not quit?

The kind of depression that comes from the emptying out of the self is a sad one. It comes out of surrender to the unnecessary. It is unnecessary to consider ourselves useless—unless we choose to be useless. It is unnecessary to think of ourselves as diminished—unless we allow ourselves to diminish in heart and mind.

The point is that there are two approaches to aging: passive aging and active aging. Passive aging gives way to the creeping paralysis of the soul that goes with the natural changes of the body. This kind of aging sees this last stage of life as a time in the throes of slow death rather than a time to live differently—and dauntlessly.

Active aging cooperates with the physical effects of age by adjusting to a change of pace. The person who is aging actively compensates for a loss of hearing by reading more, compensates for changes in eyesight by listening to tapes, and stays physically active, however limited that activity may be, rather than simply allowing the muscles of the body to go unused and therefore become useless.

Active aging requires us to go on living life to the full no matter how differently.

One of the clearest signs of healthy aging drawn from the Harvard University longitudinal Study of Adult Development[19] becomes more important as life spans increase. Lifelong learning, the study says, makes the difference between healthy and unhealthy aging. It determines the degree to which life will be satisfying to us, as well as the degree to which we will be interesting, valuable, life-giving to others.

Ongoing learning saves the aging from becoming more fossilized than transformed. The problem with aging is not age, it is petrifaction, rigidity of soul, inflexibility. Only ideas keep ideas flowing. When we close our minds to what is new, simply because we decide not to bother with it, we close our minds to our responsibility to ourselves—and to others—to keep on growing.

Surely this capacity for ongoing learning and the sense of new meaning it brings to life is not an idle gift. Surely the very fact that it develops as we grow means that it is meant for something important. And when would that be more important than when life in all its physical dimensions becomes less accessible, less doable, less desirous? Why wouldn't this capacity for learning be exactly what is needed in a generation whose responsibility is to bring the wisdom of the years to the questions of the times?

The question then is not, is the older generation capable of learning anymore? Instead, the obvious question is only, *what shall we learn now?* Shall we become even better at what we have always done, an expert in the field, a consultant in the area, an authority on the subject? Or shall we launch out into new water entirely—learn a language so we can be a help to young immigrant families in town, learn how to do woodworking and begin a small furniture restoration business out of the garage, learn how to use the computer and offer ourselves as a tutor to those who now need it in order to get the job that can actually support them? Or shall we memorize now the words of one psalm after another, one Zen koan after another, one verse of the Qur'an after another, so that those ideas ring in our soul all the way to the one same God?

A burden of these years is the fear that they bring nothing but incompetence to our once-competent selves.

A blessing of these years is that we find ourselves at a time of life when we can finally concentrate on all the things we have ever wanted to learn and know and, as a result, become an even more important, more focused, more spiritual person than we have ever really been before.

RELIGION

"Even in decline," the Tibetan master Sakya Pandita said, "the virtuous increase the beauty of their behavior. A burning stick, though turned to the ground, has its flame drawn upwards."

In the elders of every society, those flames burn clearest of all. It is of the essence of old age to ask the questions, to make sense of the answers, that we have ignored for so long, so that others can see the completion of the universal life journey of us all.

Religion is not a topic, not a course, not simply a body of beliefs. It is a process of becoming. The major error where religion is concerned is the assumption that having one dimension of it—topic, course, and body of beliefs—we have it all, and if a person does not share this dimension with everyone else, they have no real religion at all. Those judgments can be fatal—both for ourselves as well as for the effect of such ideas on others.

The fact is that religion is not one thing. It is a multi-layered phenomenon that, if successful, can bring people to the height of whatever spiritual mountain they climb. It requires commitment, education, practice, and reflection. It is none of these aspects alone. Religion is at its best when it brings all of these aspects together. But that implies a long process, a lot of learning, a great deal of reflection. In the end, as all religions know, it is in our later years that the real subject of religion—the relationship between a human being and the Creator, the evaluation of our life goals and behaviors, and the consequent surrender to the spiritual meaning of life rather than simply to the material things of life—becomes real.

Religion has various functions at various stages of life. It is a guidepost from early life through to the end. It is a direction, a map. But it is not a guarantee of anything. Religion has corrupted as much as it has saved. Clearly, there must be something more than the religion itself that must be our goal.

In early life, in youth, the function of religion is the formation of conscience. Religion sets the standards that mark the path. Every religion, according to the Universal Code of Ethics adopted at the Parliament of the World's Religions in Cape Town, South Africa, in 1999, accepts four nonnegotiables: not to steal, not to lie, not to murder, and not to exploit another sexually. Those are guidelines of the good life. There is a law above the law, we learn. And that law is the end toward which we tend.

In middle age, religion becomes a social guide. It is a measure of our relationship with others. It creates the standards that measure the quality of the soul as well as the behaviors of a person. It becomes an attitude toward life. Some things are holy, some things are not. It is the ideals to which we cling, even as we drift a bit from the moorings of our early life. All the absolutes begin to be tested. We begin to understand that religion is more a deep-down struggle to believe and to do than simply a way of acting, sterile on paper, full of thorns in the flesh.

Finally, as we grow older, when we begin that last stage of life, it is clear that behaviors and failures are not the stuff of religion much anymore. Now, the ecstasy of life and the surrender to the Mystery become the last of the revelations of religion. Now, everything we learned long ago, gave up to some degree long ago, never left completely long ago, begins to make sense. Begins to become me. Begins my new beginning as a person.

It is the older members of society who not only teach us how to live. They also teach us how to die, how to make sense of the unity between life and death, how to love life without fearing death—because we know ourselves to have been always on the way, even when we did not know where we were going

The impacting thing about religion is that it is everywhere—even in places the world never thought it would be. Like the cathedral in Moscow's Red Square. What surprised those who visited the cathedral during the Communist era in the Soviet Union was not the number of icons in gold frames or the size of the murals, beautiful as all of them were; the surprising thing about this church was that it was packed with chanting, singing, praying believers. And all of them were elderly. And this in a country whose doctrine was that belief was not to be in religion; belief was to be in the state.

In the West, religion has not been suppressed, but for many it has become some sort of social marker of the phases of life. People are baptized, married, and buried in churches, but regular attendance is less common—except, just as in pre-Glasnost Russia, for the older generation.

The relation between older generations and religion is a telling one.

Surveys in the United States show that in our own time the vast majority of Americans of all denominations, eighty percent of them, believe that the overall state of morality in the United States is bad and getting worse.[20] Many of them doubt the credibility and honesty of their clergy. And yet of ten countries polled, Americans, more than any other people, professed unquestioning belief in God, with the elderly most believing of all.[21]

The older generation everywhere, it seems, knows what younger people do not. They know that in the end it is not denominationalism, it is the spiritual life, it is faith, it is soul, that wins out.

Religion and denominationalism are not the same thing. Religion says that there is a Divine Center from which we all come and to which we will all someday return. Denominationalism says that my way is the right way to that Center.

Denominationalism, the willingness to assert or maintain the truth of my religious beliefs, wanes with age, however. Truth becomes less clear as we go along. In many ways, it is even less important than it once seemed to be. It is not facts now, dogmas now, doctrines now that we are concerned with as much as it is the nature of life, both here and now and to come. Then our questions become less about orthodoxy and more about the spiritual dimensions of life: Are we alone in this world, or have we been brought here with a purpose? Is the purpose only personal, only about me, or is it broader than that? Who am I in the world? Who am I meant to be? Are we flies on a pin of random irrationality, or are we here on the planet meant to make it better as we go?

In old age, it is not so much the way we worship, the number of church or synagogue or mosque or temple hours we clock, that counts. It is the awareness that we are all on a spiritual journey and that, however we go about making the journey, it is what becomes of us at the end of it that counts.

Then, the kind of denominationalism that makes religion a battleground begins to dim, and religion—immersion in the Mystery of life—begins to win the day.

Then the arguments about who is right and who is wrong, what is true and what is not, begin to give way to questions of what is good and what is not, what is life and what is not, what is important and what is not.

Then, in the later years, religion ceases to be simply a series of rites and rituals, of rules and answers for which I get some kind of eternal points. Religion becomes what it was always meant to be: a search and a relationship with the Spirit Who draws us on. Always on. Even to the point where "on" is unclear.

Religion is not a millstone around the neck anymore. It is the warm, soft, strong, hard awareness that yes, it has all been for something worthwhile.

A burden of these years is the fear that I have not practiced religion well enough to be worthy of the life it teaches.

A blessing of these years is the awareness that yes, it must be true: there is a God who created me and who is calling me upward, beyond myself—home.

FREEDOM

"Old age," the Austrian novelist Marie von Ebner-Eschenbach wrote, "transfigures or fossilizes."

It is a very comforting feeling to know that age does not change us. On the contrary. In some ways, we are all just getting to be more of who and what we have always been. Which means, of course, that we can decide right now what we intend to be like when we're eighty: approachable and lovable, or tyrannous and fractious. We don't, by nature, sour as we get older. The fact is that we have always been sour, but now we take the liberty of doing it with impunity. We don't get softer as we get older. We simply get to be more unabashedly loving every day of our lovable old lives. We only get to be more of what we have always wanted to be. We are free now to choose the way we live in the world, the way we relate to the world around us, the attitudes we take to life, the meaning we get out of it, the gifts we put into it. And all of them can change.

In the 1970s, when she was in her mid-thirties, Sara was part of the early group of married American women "returning to graduate school." She had two small children, a husband now professionally employed, and a farmhouse just beyond the boundary of the Big Ten university town that seethed with a new kind of energy on the other side of the mountain. She raised goats and did her own family garden, ate organic vegetables and pickled her own cucumbers. It was quite standard for the time, except that she wanted more.

She also wanted a master's degree and, eventually, a doctorate, and by the time it was over she got both. But not for any discernible academic motives.

Instead, she was more than content to teach a few undergraduate courses and then leave academia to go back to what she called "the real world." Once there, she settled down to writing columns for the smalltown newspaper that served the general public in the area.

Eventually Sara moved down south to another small town where, to all appearances, she simply replicated the life she'd had before. Her daughters moved out of the area, her husband died, and she went on working for a rural newspaper, writing columns and publishing cookbooks.

It might all classify quite neatly under "Women: standard"— except for one thing. She retired from the paper at sixty-five and went to Thailand. There, she began to teach English as a second language to young women in Bangkok as part of an international volunteer program in developing countries. Sara, "free" for the first time in her life, had tied herself down again.

To some, the situation was at best troublesome—if not downright disturbing. Why would anyone do something like this? In that place? At her age?

It takes a while to figure it out, perhaps; but it's not really all that difficult to understand. Sara didn't want to be "free." Sara wanted what she had always wanted. She wanted to be Sara. The rest of the world—the types who hype old age as some kind of adult playland—had simply misunderstood what "freedom" means.

The tendency to talk down to older people comes from stereotypes of incompetence that have been so much the caricatures we've drawn of older people once they have left the work force. Instead of honoring the wisdom and experience of the generations before us—as did the Greeks and the Romans and the American Indians, for instance—industrial/technological society infantilizes anyone whose life is no longer caught up in the skills and languages of that world. Once people can no longer talk about advertising plans or departmental goals or the job, the experience they garnered over the years is no longer a premium in the very society that produced it all. Instead, people grow useless by the end of the next quarterly report. Their so-called experience counts for nothing. They don't know the system anymore. They don't know the people. They don't even know the manager, who has also been rotated out of the organization, just as they have been. All ties are cut. All connections have expired. All experience has gone to dust.

Instead, they are "free" to be useless, the window-dressing on the society, the people left behind after the system doesn't need them anymore.

Sara did not want that kind of false freedom. Sara wanted to be Sara. She wanted to go on being more of what she had always been: productive, creative, engaged, necessary. So she went to Thailand to teach where no one would ask her age, and no one cared what it was. They simply knew that she was important to them.

She had found the secret of aging well. She redefined freedom for all the world to see.

Freedom, in childhood, may be the right to be totally self-centered. In adolescence, I am engaged in the fine art of concentrating on myself, until I know who I am and what I am capable of being. In midlife I am free to become skilled, to become prepared, to become expert, to become independent. But freedom in old age is the ability to be the best of the self I have developed during all those years. It is the freedom to gather everything I have learned up to this point and to put it to even more exciting use now. It is the freedom to give myself away to those who really need me, in ways I have never had the chance of doing before. I am free to be important to people with real needs. And with that new role in life, I become one of those rare people who know what it takes to go through life, survive its dislocations, outlive its expectations, and negotiate its shoals. Now I am free to do it not simply for my own sake—but for the sake of the world at large.

Freedom in later years is the exemption from having to live a standard-brand life. I no longer need to "fit in" to all the conventional wisdom, to the company policies and politics and political positions. I can take any position I want. I can be a socialist in a Republican club. I can be a feminist at a meeting of the pastoral planning commission. I can be an environmentalist at the oil company's stockholders meeting. I can take all the pieces of my life, weigh them carefully, and then speak the words my world needs to hear—before it's too late.

When I realize that freedom really is the right to be me, rather than someone else—perhaps for the first time in my life—the liberation of the soul begins. And with it the unshackling of the mind. I can become something new, as well as simply more of the old. Because whatever path it was that got me here is not the only path I have ever considered, ever been fascinated by, ever wanted to explore. So, why not now, when the exploration is boundaried by both common sense and a lifetime of experience?

I have the right now to explore new ideas, to think new thoughts. The ones I did not learn at home, the ones I have never dared to admit to in public. I can begin to think about God for myself, for instance. My answers will surely be as correct as anyone else's—and a great deal closer to my heart.

Finally, I am now free to become involved in life in ways I never did before when all the directions were clear and all the expectations binding and all the responsibilities defined.

Now is the time to think it all through again. Everything. God, life, work, relationships, behaviors, goals. I am free now to measure all of them against my experience, to reshape them out of my new knowledge, to try things wherever my new spiritual energy leads me, to add new ideas to the old ideas that have controlled my life for so long.

A burden of these years is to allow all the stereotypes of old age to hold me back, to hold me down, to stop the flow of life in me.

A blessing of these years is that they give me the chance to break the bounds of a past life, and to create for myself a life more suited to what I now want to be.

SUCCESS

"Though it sounds absurd," Ellen Glasgow said, "it is true to say I felt younger at sixty than I had felt at twenty."

What we are inclined to forget as we are tempted to mourn the end of middle age, the loss of youth, is that they were, in fact, quite uncomfortable times. As young people, we worried about being popular or bright or accepted. In the middle years, we worried about getting it all, having it all, enjoying it all.

But there is no doubt about it: whatever we have become at sixty, we are. The game clock has ended. Now we can just enjoy the interminable feeling of having finally survived the climb, of being free of the unceasing competition, of the unending demands for self-sacrifice. Now life is just life and no more.

Nevertheless, the conditioning goes deep. Surely there must be something we should be striving for, even now, even here. There must be something we are supposed to gain. There must be something that counts more than our own happiness or satisfaction. If not, what is there? And if not, why do I feel this way in the first place? The fact is that we get instructed in the meaning of success even while we're very young, which makes it so much more difficult to enjoy life as we get older.

We talk about teaching our children to be successful, but we really mean that we teach them to be competitive. All our lives we compete, in fact, and call it "success."

We compete for jobs and positions and promotions and salary increases. We compete with our neighbors to get a bigger house. We compete with other parents by prodding our children on to even more competition. We compete with the rest of the family to plan bigger, more exotic trips. We run every life course, we jump every hurdle, we display every ribbon and trophy and plaque the world has to give. And in the end, we're exhausted.

As a result, the ulcer and the heart condition come early. The job loses its appeal, and eventually the ones running behind catch up and overtake us. And the game is over.

But it is not so much the striving that is the problem as it is the sacrifice of all the other dimensions of life in order to achieve it. We sacrifice our own opinions, our own desires, our own interests, our own personal goals to meet the needs of people around us, and in the end, we sacrifice the burgeoning of the self for the brass rings of the social system—his better job; their family pride; the world's expectations.

Did we succeed? At what? And who knows? It all depends on what we've always thought success must be about.

The only good thing about the whole system, if we're lucky, is that the role will end before we do. And probably sooner than we think. Then, we will begin the task of rethinking everything we ever thought success was all about.

Retirement is the counterculture of the culture. It says that just being alive and learning to live well is sign in itself to the rest of humanity of the quintessential goodness of life. The purpose of a job is to make a living, not to make a life. Making a life is something we're meant to do beyond the role. This is the part of life in which we work at succeeding at all the other dimensions of what it means to be alive.

The questions with which we are faced at retirement are *not* the questions this society instructs us to answer as we seek societal "success."

Did we succeed at making the family a "family"? If not, there are still years left to do it. We can call the kids instead of waiting for them to come to us. We can send cards and offer our car and take the grandchildren to the zoo now.

Did we succeed at being a good neighbor? If not, there are people on the block who need someone to pick up things at the store for them, people down the hall who would love to go out for a drive, people who would love to have someone to play cards with, to go to the show with, to share simple food and long conversation.

Did we succeed at developing a genuine spiritual life, the kind in which the presence of God dominates our whole existence, above and beyond worship attendance on holy days and liturgical events? If not, we can join a prayer group now or a reading group or a social action group and do what needs to be done to leave the Earth a better place than when we arrived on it.

Did we succeed in living gently on Earth, on creating a balance in our lives of time with nature, time with people, time with God, time for reflection, time for a new kind of personal development? If not, it's time to plan our days rather than simply have them slip by unnoticed.

Did we succeed in learning how to be happy ourselves by walking the dog, making jewelry, learning to fish, restoring wood—doing something that we do only because we love doing it?

Did we succeed at developing the kind of interior life it takes to weather the external demands of life?

Did we succeed at becoming a person—a real person? A person who is real!

In the end, it becomes so clear: success is a much simpler thing than they ever told us. It has to do with having the basics, with learning to be happy, with getting in touch with our spiritual selves, with living a balanced life, doing no harm, doing nothing but good. The only test of the good life here is happiness.

The burden of false success is that it creates an artificial standard that follows us through our entire lives, leaves us in fear, leaves us in a state of perpetual discontent, too tight to enjoy retirement, too invested in the elements of life that do not last.

The blessing of real success lies in the fact that sometime in life we come to the point where we never overemphasize any one side of it again. Instead, we come to live easily and fully in all aspects of it.

TIME

"It takes a long time," Pablo Picasso wrote, "to become young."

The beauty of the later years, in other words, is that if we have learned through life to trust our own insights at least as much as we trust the insights we have been taught, we find ourselves at the end of a very long life with a very young soul.

Time has done for us what needs to be done. We have deepened as people. We have broadened as personalities. We have softened as thinkers. We have abandoned arrogance and authoritarianism for reflection on new ideas and respect for others. We now see newly, clearly, what in some ways we have never seen before. If we watch older people closely, the free ones, the ones who let life come to them rather than trying to wrench it to themselves, we can see it happen right in front of us.

Thomas was a handsome man. The fine-trimmed white beard, the dark deep-set eyes of a philosopher and the enigmatic smile that hinted of the Puck in him suggested a more baronial era. But he was not a baron, he was a working artist.

"Just work," the sign on his studio wall read. And, indeed, every morning at 6 a.m., for over twenty-five years, he went to his studio to do the hard, solitary processes of the master potter, an ancient skill to which he himself had added much over the years. His pieces, huge and classic, modern and gleaming, stood in galleries and museums around the world, from the Vatican in Rome, to the Victoria and Albert in England, to the Smithsonian in the United States. And every year he added astonishingly unique pieces to the collection.

He lived life smothered in clay dust and smudged with glaze. His studio was powdered white and stacked with compounds of ore from Nova Scotia and dried leaves from China, cluttered with bags of clay and hung with racks of greenware awaiting the kiln. One narrow path led from the door to his worktable, another from the table to the wheel. That was all he needed. That was all he wanted.

His art was his life—past and future—and the future, the desire to make the perfect pot, was his obsession. "It is the curse, the blessing, of the beginner's mind," he said. "You never achieve; you simply go on learning, go on trying, in the hope that someday whatever is supposed to happen will happen."

Time hung heavy on his shoulders. He feared it. There was so much he had to do yet, he said. He was already seventy-eight, a bit worried about the weight on his arms of the big pieces, and planning a major retrospective of his work in two years, when he would be eighty. He was, he said, "far from finished." And every year he produced a new and different set of molds, more dazzling and more unusual glazes.

Then, one night, he fell in the hall outside his room and bled. When the diagnosis came it shattered more than Thomas.

"Inoperable," they said. "Weeks," they announced. "How do you feel?" he was asked. "Disappointed," he said.

Time had had her way with him. But not before he had lived long enough, worked long enough, to release the beginner in himself again and again. Thomas had raced time—and lost. As do we all. But not before he had learned to play with life. To be more than potter. To deny all the old ideas the right to choke the new insights out of him.

Time, it is clear, has its way with all of us. Eventually. If we will only allow it.

Nothing weighs more heavily on age than time. Nothing has more meaning. Time is now everything—the only thing—that is left in life. Time is, suddenly, not for wasting. Now time becomes, with a kind of ruthless honesty, what it has always been: life's most precious commodity. The only difference is that, finally, we know it.

But time is not one-dimensional. Time is a great deal more than simply "passing." It has a function in life like little else.

When we are young, time goes very slowly, not because time is anything but regular but because we are always rushing then. Living in the moment is not the mark of youth. Instead, the young are always on the way to somewhere else. They have no patience for now—because they live their lives trying to get beyond the confines of now to the possibilities of soon. They want to get to be older, to be independent, to be important, to be wealthy, to be somebody. They are immersed in wanting.

The old, on the other hand, have long ago exhausted both the wanting and the going and the striving. They are immersed in being. Being alive, being healthy, being present to the moment, being who they are, being happy, being young again in delight and in vision.

To be beyond the years when getting established and getting secure are the focal points of life leaves us with the awesome possibility of living. Simply living. Now it isn't contacts or credentials that count, it's time. Time to live the rest of life with fresh presence and unworn understanding.

Time ages things—and not simply ourselves. It ages our memories and allows us the joy of culling them. It ages our irritations and allows us the relief of ignoring them. It ages our relationships and gives us the comfort of surety.

Time deepens things, too. It gives us the luxury of taking so much for granted now. It may be cold today but, patience, it won't be too long and the sun will return. The grandchild may be crying now, but she will smile again in the morning. The neighbors may be feuding with one another again, but they will all get over it as they have so many times before. Whatever the many deaths of the day, resurrection is coming. We know that it will because—give it time—it always has before and it will now as well.

Time ripens things. It brings everything to fulfillment. We ourselves become more mature, more accepting, more serene. We have survived so much already, what can possibly destroy our equanimity now? We have seen it all—war, loss, pain, the decline of systems, the breakup of relationships, the crises in business, the scarcity of money, the horror of debt. And lo, here we are still. Here we are yet. Here we are. And that is enough for us to have it all.

Now we live in the intensity of time, and with a new sense of eternity. And it fills us with a sense of urgency. It rises in us like great waves of emotional shock: who has ever seen the grass so green? Who has ever watched the roses bloom like this? Who has ever tasted the calm of evening before this night, or smelled the sweet morning air? And if it has all happened before, where was I when it happened?

Time is a wondrous thing, if only I fill it well. If I do not allow the passing of time to diminish my spirit but, instead, see it as a call to live life to the dregs—being, like Thomas, my best and developing and life-loving self to the end. Then time is my friend, not my enemy. It gives me a heightened sense of life. It urges me on to discover it all. It marks the fullness of life, its mellowing, and it releases in me the self that has been coming into existence from the beginning. It is a new kind of life.

Now, too, I have the quiet time, the solitary time, to think it all through—everywhere I've been, everyone I've known, everything I've done in life with all the glories and all the sad mistakes, all the successes and all the personal failures—and to be glad for all of it. There is not one of them that did not teach me something about life. There is not one of them that did not make me stronger. And they are all me. They are everything I bring to this time now—when the only question yet to answer in life is what I have become.

A burden of these years is to allow time to hang heavy on my hands, to simply sit and wait for life to be over— as the Irish say, "knocking another day out of it till the great day comes."

A blessing of these years is to realize what an important and lively time this final period is. I can, if I will, bring it all together, into the final and the very best of me.

WISDOM

"In youth we learn," Marie von Ebner-Eschenbach wrote when she was seventy-five years old, "in age we understand."

Clearly, here was a woman who understood the function of age, the role of the elderly.

Understanding is the bedrock of a society. It enables us to see why we do what we do, to realize why we cannot do what we want to do in all instances. It is in the development of understanding for the next generation, in the cocreation of the world, that the older generation has so serious a role to play.

The service that the whole world needs from the elders is not the service of hours spent and time put in and documents finished and machines fixed. There are untold numbers of people who can do all of those things.

No, the service of the elders is not a service of labor, it is a service of enlightenment, of wisdom, of discernment of spirits. Only the carriers of generations past can give us those things, because wisdom is what lasts after an experience ends. We cannot expect wisdom as a wholesale item of the young, then, because they simply have not lived long enough or through enough to have been able to amass much of it.

Oddly enough, this period in life when we finally get to the point that we really understand some things about living well is when we feel most out of it. It is, far too often, exactly the time when people who know more than they have ever known begin to feel useless. Out of the mainstream of the middle years, not going into the office or the store or the bus barn anymore, not responsible for the meetings or the committees or the children or the family or the business, we begin to doubt that there is any role left for us in life. After all, everything that ever gave us status or influence at all has simply dried up, disappeared, or moved on.

The children are off on their own now. They call, they visit, but they never ask for much help anymore. They manage their own families and money now. They aren't looking for our advice.

The company sends newsletters, of course, but our names are never in them now. We hardly understand the new language they're using, let alone feel like we're still a part of it. We actually have no idea what they're talking about in those newsletters anymore. We don't say so, of course, but down deep we know that we've lost touch.

We hear the bustle on the street outside, we hear the clicking of heels on the steps in the hallway, but no one stops to tell us where they're going or where they've been.

Clearly our role, if there is one, has changed. But to what? For what purpose? And if we have no role at all, what's left for

us in this world? What are we to anyone now that we are nothing at all of the things we once thought were so important?

In fact, the moment of apparent disengagement is exactly
the moment when we become most important to the world
around us. We are beyond the stage of being simply another
replaceable part in life now. We and everything we believe in
or know about or understand cannot be replaced. These un-
derstandings are uniquely ours. These ideas that have taken a
lifetime to develop cannot be substituted for by any simple
technical routine. These are the things of the soul.

Our role now is to be what we have discovered about life.
Our responsibility is wisdom. Only those who have lived in
this society long enough really stand to have the insight to
know what it needs, to point out what it doesn't.

If nothing else, those who are beyond the pressures of the
workforce, for instance, are most likely to understand the effects of it on the human spirit. At the very least, then, it is
the older generation which is able to show us all another way
to live.

Americans, researchers tell us, have much less reflection
time than almost any other culture in the modern world.
The United States is the most vacation-starved country in the
Western world. A minimum of several weeks of rest and vacation is standard in much of Europe, for example—whereas
many Americans have barely two weeks paid vacation time
each year.

According to Joe Robinson, author of *Work to Live* and
founder of the Work to Live Campaign in the United States,
"in terms of work time logged, Americans work a full two
months more a year than Germans do," for instance.

The elderly, by living at a more leisurely pace, by taking the time to read again, to pursue new questions, by involving themselves in the discussions of the day, have the opportunity to bring to us a wisdom that comes from experience.

Older people have what this world needs most: the kind of experience that can save the next generation from the errors of the one before them. This is a generation, for instance, that knows the unfathomable horrors of mass genocide and holocaust. This generation knows that war does nothing but plant the seeds of the next one. This generation knows that there is no such thing as "rugged individualism" anymore; we are in this changing world together. The older generation knows that the only thing that is good for any of us in the long run is what is good for all of us right now. That's wisdom. Wisdom is not insisting on the old ways of doing things. It is the ability to make ancient truth the living memory of today.

Only the elderly have lived through both the good and the bad decisions of the past. It is they, then, who have the wisdom to alert us to alternatives, to evaluate present choices from the perspective of history.

The role of the elders is to bring their wisdom to the decision-making tables of the world where, too commonly now, only pragmatism reigns. The world needs women and men who will question whether what can be done, should be done. It is the experience of the elders that tells the world that force is not the only way to solve a problem. They know, having seen Germany and Japan suffer from their own militarism, that even force may not be the best way to achieve security. They know, too, that money may not be the answer to a problem. They know what happens to the marrow of a country when corruption swamps integrity and the thirst for power turns into paranoia as it did in the McCarthy era.

Remove the public face of the older generation and you remove the memory of the world, the sensitivities of the ages. Inventing the nuclear bomb was easy. To refrain from using it, however, is the preeminent need of the time. And that demands great wisdom.

Wisdom is not the quality of being wedded to the past. Wisdom is the capacity to be devoted to its ideals. As the Japanese poet Basho wrote, "I do not seek to follow in the footsteps of those of old. I seek only what they sought."

And why must the elders in a society immerse themselves in the issues of the time? If for no other reason than that they are really the only ones who are free to tell the truth. They have nothing to lose now: not status, not striving, not money, not power. They are meant to be the prophets of a society, its compass, its truth-tellers.

No, older people are not useless in a society—unless they choose to be. But to relinquish the position of seer and sage in a society rife with technicians and bureaucrats is to abandon the world we made. Now is our time to evaluate what we have done, what we have lost, what we are losing—and to spare no efforts to make it known. It is the older generation that must turn the spotlight back on our best ideals when the lights of the soul go dim. Before it is too late.

A burden of these years is to accept the notion that nothing can be done to save a people when a younger generation is in charge.

A blessing of these years is to have the opportunity to take on the role of thinker, of philosopher, of disputant, of interrogator, of spiritual guide in a world racing to nowhere, with no true human goal and no lived wisdom in sight.

SADNESS

"Old wood best to burn, old wine to drink, old friends to trust, and old authors to read," said Francis Bacon.

And he was surely right, at least from one perspective. There is something about getting older that tempts us to settle down a bit. We begin to run the ruts in the road, not because we cannot find our way to other paths, other places, other people but because we really don't want to make the effort it takes to do it. To meet new people, to develop new ideas, to talk about new things, to learn new patterns not only takes effort, it also demands new attention. The thought of the familiar, on the other hand, comforts us. It assures us that life as we have known it is still there, still stable, still secure.

So we settle into a routine of friends and foods and places and plans and ideas. It's easier. More than the fact that it's easy, it is also fulfilling. These things are our identity as well as our pleasure. They say who we are, who we have always been, where we belong and why.

But there is a cost to be paid for settling in to be totally and only what we have always been. The cost of familiarity is the angst of loss, the anxiety that comes with feeling more and more alone as the old commonplaces of life disappear: the neighborhood bar that is no longer there, the sports club that has closed, the old clothing store that knew both our sizes and our tastes. As one thing after another goes, there is our growing awareness that we are becoming a world unto ourselves, whom no one knows anymore.

No wonder there is a natural melancholy that sets in as the years pass by. The world around us begins to change and, little by little, the world that shaped us fades away, without so much as a notice, with hardly a nod. But then one day, in a rush, all the beauties of those years come roaring through us in an emotional whirlwind. The problem is that nobody cares about them now but us. Those years have taken with them a part of ourselves. Is it to be mourned—or celebrated—for its disappearance?

The life that's gone is the life that shaped us. And what makes us sad is not so much that it isn't here anymore—it's the wondering whether what this life formed in us is still there or not.

The remembrance of the days we learned to kneel down to say our night prayers and stand up straight to sing our hymns has nothing of absolute value to maintain the present, of course. But what is worth wondering about, perhaps, is whether or not we still have any of that early piety in us. The pain that comes with the remembrance of piety lost is a good kind of pain. It means that there is something in us yet that holds on to the innocence of childhood. We have not become nearly as jaded, nearly as unbelieving as we thought we were. We have moved now to the hard-won truth of hard-won virtue, the kind of virtue a person learns the hard way. Only after the rules are broken—after we stop worrying about whether or not the passions of youth endanger salvation—are the lessons really learned. If we forget the presence of God in our lives, we know now, we find ourselves terribly alone. No doubt about it—there are moments from the past which, when they flash back, carry the sting of new awareness.

The sadness comes to tell us, too, that there is a value to age, including our own. What ages well, we know from wines and cheeses, are the ones that have the most quality, the greatest flavor, the staying power over time. Aging is not enough in itself. Aging well is the real goal of life. To allow ourselves to age without vitality, without energy, without purpose, without growth is simply to get old rather than to age well as we go.

Aging is the process by which we face the tasks of every level of life. And the ones we fail at, or postpone as we go, are always unfinished business, left to be resolved in the years to come.

Life is meant to form us in independence, usher us into an adulthood that begins in apprenticeship and ends in mastery, and then, those tasks accomplished, to bring us to the acme of integrity, of wisdom, of eldership in the community of the world. It is a process of ripening as we go, getting stronger, getting more caring, becoming more procreative, sharing more wisdom as we grow—so that those who come after us can walk a clearer path.

The sadness of friends lost, then, is the sadness that comes when the companionship they brought us through each of the earlier stages of life, laughing and learning all the way, begins to unravel. We lose contact, they move away, they disappear. They leave us thrown back on our own devices. Or maybe we left them for shinier lures, only to discover later that there was nothing in life that could match such fellowship. Any mountain can be climbed, we come to understand, as long as we are tethered to someone at least as good as ourselves. The images come and go through the years and with them the remembrance of love unearned.

Finally, we remember the great heroes, the noble ideas, the fine deeds that we ourselves inherited from the past. They focused our hearts on higher goals when we were young. They filled us with the notions of the grandeur of the soul. They acted like a magnet on our heart. What happened to those? What happened to us? Were we up to the level of any of them at all? The sadness comes because we know we wanted to be as pure, as fearless, as true in our own lives as they in theirs. But somewhere along the line, life became more absorbing, more overwhelming, more complex than that. And so now, in the time that is left, life is not over. There is unfinished business aplenty to do, too many things left unsaid, too much teaching yet to be done if we are ever to do our part in making our world as good as those heroes of earlier generations made theirs.

A burden of these years is the desire to give in to the natural sadness that comes with the shifting journey through life, to cling to it in ways that make living in the present a dour and depressing prospect.

A blessing of these years is the realization that there is still so much for us to do that we have no time, no right, to be sad.

DREAMS

"In a dream you are never eighty," Anne Sexton wrote.

Whatever happens to the body, what toll age takes on the physical, the spirit does not grow old. In our dreams, in the way we ourselves see ourselves, we are forever becoming. Our dreams are always the vision of a younger self, a self-contained, energetic, self-determining person with a will of steel.

Our dreams reveal to us the basic truth of life: years are biological; the spirit is eternal. The number of our years do not define us. There is in the human being a life force that never dies. It is the life force that proves to us that age does not fossilize us. Down deep, where our souls live, we stay forever young. It is this surging, driving force that brings us to the bar of life every day of our lives, whatever our age, however much we have been through, prepared to live life to the hilt again. It is only the cold, clear light of dawn that damps it, the fear in ourselves that the years have taken us beyond the right to be active. It is our own fault if we refuse to think again all the great ideas of life—and our own position on each of them.

The person within the person, the personality and the soul within an aging body stays always alert, ever dynamic. Even when we find ourselves less physically active than we may once have been, the mind wrestles with the ideas of the soul, the heart reviews over and over again every emotional moment of life, every major turn along the way. We are forever in motion, as long as we live, one way or another.

To stay alive, fully alive, then, we must open ourselves to life's eternal dream.

We must dream to be better people tomorrow than we were today. We do not have the right to give up growing just because age is assumed by many to have eclipsed the possibility. But that means that we must be willing to rethink all the ideas that have kept us bound until this moment. Are they still believable? Do we ourselves still believe them? And if we do not, what does that mean in regard to what we say to those younger people who have been influenced by these ideas because of us?

One of the problems we face in the modern world is that we are more fascinated with the technological than we are with the spiritual. We are very good at reporting every scientific or technical wonder the world has ever spawned. But there are other elements of life that are even more important, more profound, more impacting on human society, more hidden in plain sight, and we are inclined to miss them entirely. One of them has special meaning to the aging. One of them shows us that the dreams that determine the ultimate quality of our lives never die, are never too late to be grasped. It is the ability of humans to change their minds, to begin again, to start over, to be someone else.

At the age of eighty-one, Robert McNamara, past secretary of defense under John F. Kennedy and Lyndon B. Johnson, told the public that he had thought it over and could no longer support U.S. involvement in Vietnam. Nor could he condone his own part in it.

What's more, McNamara, after years out of public service, wrote a book and cooperated in the filming of Errol Morris's prize-winning documentary *The Fog of War*. Not only was the report itself, made so close to the event itself, unusual, but so was the fact that the man who made it was one of the chief architects of the American conduct of the war in Vietnam. Robert McNamara, past president of Ford Motor before he became U.S. Secretary of Defense, had reflected again on what he had done in the past, why he had done it, what he thought about it then and now and came to a startling conclusion: "Although we sought to do the right thing—and believed we were doing the right thing—in my judgment," he writes, "hindsight proves us wrong."[22]

This analysis, weighed against a deeper dream of human virtue and change of perspective, took place twenty-five years after the end of the war. Furthermore, other leaders of the era, all high-ranking and all as involved in the conduct of the war as he was, refused to engage in similar conversations either with the Vietnamese of the era, or even in conversations among themselves in the United States.

The very act of reviewing one's own values, then and now, stands as a marker for us all. It reminds us that it is possible to learn as we go through life. It is even more important to be open to doing it and willing to report it. Life grows us. Life shapes us. Life converts us. Life opens us as we age to think differently, even about ourselves.

Whatever our physical age, we must go on dreaming of the desirable so that we can do our bit to make it happen. To simply withdraw from the arena of ideas, from public discourse on public issues, from the value formation of the young—to shrug our shoulders and say, "I don't know" or, worse, "I don't care about those things anymore"—is to abandon the young to the mercy of their own ideas without the benefit of experience to guide them.

We must allow ourselves to dream about what life could really be like if enough of us demanded that it were. But to do that means to open for examination all the assumptions that have driven the world to this point. All of them.

In our dreams lies our unfinished work for the world. What we hope for is a guide to our present obligations to bring wisdom to the world. It is, of course, a wisdom derived from experience of all ilk: from our mistakes and our ideals, from our losses and our insights, from pain and from the little joys of our own past life and present situation.

> *A burden of these years is that we come to think that our dreaming days are over. Then we become mired in the past. We refuse to grow. We make past mistakes the definition of our entire life.*

> *A blessing of these years is the power to dream and the freedom it takes to bring to the awareness of our world—however small, however boundaried it may be—the voice of reflection, of reason, of feeling, of penetrating awareness that comes with having been wrong and setting out to right it.*

LIMITATIONS

"Old age is not a disease," Maggie Kuhn said. "It is strength and survivorship."

When we ignore the fact that all of us are on an inexorable journey to our own old age, we miss the gift of years. We miss the profound insight that we are never too young to begin to see ourselves as old, to imagine ourselves as now, at this moment, shaping what we will be in years to come—as well as the way we will become it. All of us will sooner or later arrive at the point where we are beginning to imagine ourselves entering the final stages of our lives and asking ourselves, seriously, quietly, what kind of person we want to be then, so that we can begin to be that person now. If we're lucky, we meet older people who challenge us into that moment simply by being themselves—something we do not expect at one age or another, and certainly not at a later age, to happen. Even to us.

If anyone proves the point, it is surely Maggie Kuhn. She looked not like your typical main speaker at major health-care events across the country. She was small, frail as a bird, hardly able to be seen above the speaker's stand in front of her. And she was a woman.

There was a lot of talk about women in the 1980s, of course, but you still didn't see many of them in the public arena. Maggie Kuhn hardly seemed the type to be the pacesetter of a whole new public life for older women. By the end of every presentation, however, people—men as well as women—came leaping to their feet cheering, applauding, calling her name.

Maggie Kuhn, born in 1905, was the founder of the Gray Panthers movement. Having retired from seminary work in the Presbyterian Church at the age of sixty-five, she founded what would, in fifteen short years, become one of the most influential groups of retired people the world had ever known. She had dedicated the group to nursing-home reform, to the elimination of ageism, and to the eradication of the social concept of "disengagement," the notion that older people should be beyond, outside, disengaged from the public arena. On the contrary.

Thanks to the Gray Panthers, legislation easing the lot of older Americans, promising them economic support and breaking down the barriers of ageism, was already moving through Congress and, best of all, alive in the public mind.

With Maggie Kuhn, a whole new population speaking out against ageism began to emerge. The elderly were alive and well and on the move.

We are their inheritors.

But is it realistic to think that the elderly elderly—eighty-year-olds—can possibly have any real effect on public issues? How can those who are almost by definition limited in one way or another be expected to be the shapers of a new society for themselves, let alone for anyone else? They wear hearing aids. They get cataract surgery. They don't drive much anymore. Well, maybe. But what they can do, they do with increasing amounts of energy and intention.

They know enough about computers to contact one another. They know enough about business, given the fact that so many of them have run one, to organize. They know enough about government, since so many of them have been involved in it at one level or the other, to pool all of that experience, all of that passion, all of that commitment to change politics—whatever the limitations of each of them might be separately. "Old people," Kuhn said, "constitute America's biggest untapped and undervalued human energy source."

More than that, however, they teach the rest of the population, all of its various age groups, something about the power of limitations. No, they aren't as young as they once were, and they don't walk as fast—if at all. They may not organize major political events or societal fund-raisers. But what they do for us, no one else can do. They make us rethink the entire function and meaning of "limitation."

Limitations—those physical boundaries that the old reach before the rest of the world—are only that, elders show us. They are boundaries, not barriers. They limit us—they take time and energy, yes—but they do not stop us unless we decide to be stopped. In fact, limitations in one area simply make us develop in another. If your legs are weak, then getting in and out of a wheelchair will only make your arms stronger. If your hearing is impaired, you will begin to write more letters. Limitations, at any age and every age, call out something in us that we never considered before.

They also alert us to the needs of others. It takes limitations to teach us to be sensitive to their needs. Once our own eyes are not as good as they once were, we want visual aids for everyone. And we will do everything we can to get them.

Being limited gives us an opportunity to learn both humility and patience. We aren't as arrogant anymore as we used to be. But we're more tenacious than ever. Because we know how hard it is to get out of a chair, walk across a room and make ourselves supper, we have learned to stop expecting instant results. We can wait. We can try again. Just as we have learned to do routine physical things differently. Now, we can keep attempting to find another way to get a Congressperson on the phone, to launch a petition, to get a letter to the editor published in the paper.

Finally, limitations invite others to get involved as well. We create community out of the needs of the others and the gifts we can bring to them while they, in turn, enrich us.

We become prophets of the poor and unknown, the limited and unloved, the needy and forgotten. We become connected to the rest of the human race, all of whom are just as limited as we are, whether they know it yet or not.

Limitations are the mutual stock of the human race. By helping ourselves we also help others. By helping others we extend our own reach.

The truth is that we are only as limited as we want to be. When we define ourselves only by our limitations, we fail to see to what greater things those limitations are calling us for. What made Maggie Kuhn a modern hero was the way she transcended both age and physical boundaries to be the strong, thinking, visionary person the world badly needed.

She was the essence of vision. She was the exemplar of experience in action. She was brave and smart and persistent. She was everyone's favorite grandmother, everyone's idol, everyone's alter ego. She was what we all wanted to see come to life in ourselves as the years went by.

Age and limitations are no excuse for being a nonperson in a world that needs icons of truth and courage, vision and possibility as never before. She was what the world wanted in the elderly: wisdom, truth, and the sign of a better future for us all.

A burden of these years is the possibility that we might succumb to our limitations as if they were the real definition of age, rather than an aspect of everyone's life.

A blessing of these years is that we know at last what really matters, and the world is waiting to hear it, if only we will make the effort and don't give in to our limitations.

SOLITUDE

"For a younger person," Carl Jung taught, "it is almost a sin—and certainly a danger—to be too much occupied with himself. But for the aging person it is a duty and a necessity to give serious attention to himself. After having lavished its light upon the world, the sun withdraws its rays in order to illumine itself."

Carl Jung, the great psychologist of the inner life, brought to human awareness the notion that life develops in stages, some of them more centered on the outside world, others of them focused almost entirely on interiority, on reflection, on the search for meaning. The end stage of life, it seems, has something to do with making sense out of everything that has gone before it.

It requires a capacity for questions about what happened to us as we went through life to come to this point. And why. And how we handled what happened to us. And, most of all, perhaps, what it means to us now. Clearly, it also requires the courage to brave the answers to questions like that.

But that is not done in chaos. It can be done only in the

center of the soul and with brutal honesty. Now is the time to stop excusing ourselves. This is the time to drain the dross of life and to celebrate its victories over the self—even the victories unknown to those who think they know us best. Certainly the ones that made new and better people out of us.

Indeed, that kind of thinking and reflecting is only really done well when it is done alone, in solitude. When we find ourselves alone, all the people we have ever known, still very much alive in us, come back again to help us see where we have been, to understand what we have become, to help us chart what it will take to make these final years our best ones.

"They're all gone now," the woman said. "My husband's been dead almost ten years now and my son and his family are in California." So was there no one with her at all? "No, no one is here anymore," she said. "Sometimes my sister and her daughter come to visit. And I go there, too—once or twice a year. But it's too long a trip to go often." The words would likely be overlooked, perhaps, as an unfortunate description of a unique situation, if they weren't so common. It's not the rare elderly person who lives alone nowadays. It's almost all of them. Everywhere.

Aloneness is the new monastery of the elderly.

Sometimes in life aloneness is a conscious choice. There are, after all, a growing number of singles of all ages living alone now. They like the freedom of being on their own. They want the experience of taking care of a place they can call completely their own. They are following jobs that will be good on their resumes, and so they live alone till this position leads to other jobs in other places. Or, they are in between, like in between the family's home and settling down to create their own. For them solitude is not a way of life.

In old age, however, aloneness is, more than likely, not chosen at all. It is simply thrust upon us. Then, it brings with it none of the romantic images of a log cabin in the woods or a loft apartment in the city or a condo on the beach somewhere. Now it is only an empty house or a small apartment in the new housing complexes for the elderly that have become so common with the rise of the nuclear family. Few members of most families continue to live in the same neighborhood or town anymore where they grew up. Corporations took care of that.

The problem with solitude is that we often confuse it with aloneness or isolation. Isolation means that we are cut off from the rest of the world by circumstances over which we have no control; people don't respond to us, for instance, no matter how hard we try to make contact with them. We live outside the mainstream, on a farm out in the prairie, perhaps. We are too sick, too lame, too shy, too angry, too far away from people to have any kind of social life.

Isolation, in other words, is either separation or alienation from the world around us. Solitude is something quite different.

Solitude is chosen. It is the act of being alone in order to be with ourselves. We seek solitude for the sake of the soul. Even with easy access to other people, we take time to be by ourselves, to close out the rest of the world, to concentrate on the inside of us rather than wrestle with everything going on around us.

Solitude opens us to the wonders of a world without noise, a world without clutter, a world purged of the social whirl. At least for awhile. At least long enough to immerse ourselves in the balm of simply being.

When the outside world, its clatter and volume, its pressures and pesterings go silent, then we are alone with ourselves. Then the silence outside ourselves enables us to go inside ourselves.

In solitude we wait for all the noise to quiet in order to find out what we are really thinking about, what we are really saying to ourselves underneath all the layers of other people's messages that threaten to smother the words of our own heart.

Solitude empties us of the detritus that has built up in us over the years and lets us find the deep, calm place that makes aging such a serene part of life.

It's in the center of the soul where the unspoken in us runs deep. Here are the ideas we long ago refused to allow ourselves to think and yet could never not think. Here, too, are the ideas we never knew we had. Now, in solitude, we have the opportunity to take them out, turn them over in our mind, look at them, own them—or disown them. Once and for all. They are the parts of us that cry for some kind of settlement, not with anyone else, but within ourselves. Is the old anger worth it? Was the loss really a loss in the long run? If we didn't do what we wanted to do, in what way did we grow instead? It's in solitude where we come to peace with ourselves and the life that is behind us now.

We find ourselves back in contact with our past in a new way. We are beyond it now, not able to be hurt by it now, no longer humiliated by it now. Whatever we have done, wherever we have been in life, we are what we are because of it. Stronger because of it, perhaps.

It is here in the well of the self that our unfinished self, our real self, lies waiting for attention. No, there is nothing we can change about what was—except the way we look at it. No, there is little that we can change about what is—except the way we look at it. If there is something in us that has yet to be grappled with, this is the grappling hour.

Solitude is not a way of running away from life, from the aging process, from our feelings. On the contrary. This is the time we sort them out, air them, get over them, and go on without the burden of yesterday.

There is a life to be lived in the last years that ought not to end infected by what went before this. We have an obligation now to live well with the people around us who are making this new life possible. We owe them the best we have. And the best that is in us is what is undefiled by the past.

Solitude is what forces us to assess our present as well as to review our past. Are we living now the happiest way we can in the circumstances we're in? That responsibility will be ours to the end. Solitude is what enables us to illuminate for ourselves whatever it is in us that is making that impossible.

A burden of these years is that we fail to understand that solitude is the gift that comes naturally to those who take the time and the space to explore their core.

A blessing of these years is that solitude is their natural state, the gift of reflection that makes the present a contented place to be.

PRODUCTIVITY

"The answer to old age," Leon Edel wrote, "is to keep one's mind busy and to go on with one's life as if it were interminable. I always admired Chekhov for building a new house when he was dying of tuberculosis."

To insist on living until we die may be one of life's greatest virtues. It is easy at any age simply to stop, to be satisfied with what is, to refuse to be more. But when we go on working—at something, for some reason, for someone, for something greater than ourselves—when we go on giving ourselves away right to the very end, we have lived a full life. That is, in fact, the very definition of fullness of life. For some people, it means watering the flowers every day of their lives. For others, it means continuing to write, to practice the piano, to prepare to make the world a better place before we go because we have been here.

What it does *not* mean is that we will become accustomed, happy even, with allowing ourselves to go to seed, to grow dry and brittle from the inside out, to stop thinking when it is precisely thought that the world needs most. Instead, it is the fine art of going on, of making life something I need to get up for every day. It is a sign to the world around us that we have each and all been put here to make this world different than it was before we came.

Retirement has nothing to do with whether we work or whether we don't. It has something to do only with the kind of work we do and the reason we do it.

The difference between the kind of work I do in my early years and the work I do in my later years is obvious. The purpose of retirement is not to free us from working. It is to free us from being chained to it like road gangs to gravel beds. It is not meant to be a punishment for sin, "doomed to earn our living by the sweat of our brow," as the old spirituality manuals implied, unconscious, it seems, that humans were told to "till the land and keep it" long before sin ever entered the world. Instead, work is meant to be a fulfillment of our very selves and our purpose for being alive.

Work is a necessary dimension of the spiritual life, then. Without it, "tilling and keeping" the globe, tending to our own garden of paradise, is impossible. We are not here simply to live off the fruits of the Earth. We are here to replant them, to prune them, to till them, to tend them as well.

The work we do and the way we do it is what we leave behind for generations to come.

Work is not slavery, then. Work is creativity. It is the expression of ourselves that no one else can duplicate. It is totally unique, completely our own. No two people sweep a floor the same way. No two people plant flowers the same way. Our work is as distinct as our fingerprints, as originally configured as our DNA. It is the stamp we put upon the world, the mark we leave behind.

But in that case, retirement does not free us from the responsibility to go on tending the world. What's more, the work we do after we retire is not useless, valueless work, simply because it is not paid labor. On the contrary.

This may, in fact, be the first moment in our lives when we are really free to choose work that brings out the best in us and so brings out the best in the world around us. We become co-creators of the world.

Then the only question is, what work will we do? And the answer to that is, whatever work needs to be done where we are! There is hardly a school in the country that would not welcome volunteer tutors. Every nonprofit needs those who are willing to make the organization work without demanding to get paid. Where is the city neighborhood that could not use flowers or street sweeping or some dedicated litter patrol?

These years are for the development of the soul. These are the years we learn to paint, or go back to playing an instrument again, or become a Little League coach, or visit nursing homes so that the people there, so many of them alone in the world, have someone to talk to about important things.

A burden of these years is that we begin to think of ourselves as superfluous simply because we are no longer tied down to a corporate schedule anymore.

A blessing of these years is that they enable us to change our part of the world in ways that are as expressive of us as they are good for others.

MEMORIES

"What makes old age hard to bear," W. Somerset
Maugham wrote, "is not the failing of one's faculties,
mental and physical, but the burden of one's memories."

The task, of course, is to refuse to make our memories a
burden. Instead, the goal is to give them the kind of meaning
that makes them precious rather than painful. What we often
fail to realize is that memory is a mental function, yes, but it is
also a choice. We do get to decide which of our memories of a
particular time, or person, or place, or moment may shape our
life in the present moment.

Memory is one of the most powerful functions of the human mind. It is also one of life's most determining ones. What
goes on in memory has a great deal to do with what goes on in
us all our lives. Memory is a wild horse, unbridled, riderless,
maverick. It takes us often where we would not go, or takes
us back over and over again to where we cannot stay, however
much we wish we could. So, it leaves us always in one state
or the other, one place or the other, leaves us either pining or

confused, leaves us in either case in a world unfinished in us.

It is the unfinishedness that is the price we pay for growing always older.

The young hear memory in the voice of their elders and, delighted by these voices from the past or bored by them, too often miss the content behind the content. Memory is not about what went on in the past. It is about what is going on inside of us right this moment. It is never idle. It never lets us alone. It is made up of the stuff of life in the process of becoming the grist of the soul.

There is an energy in memory that is deceiving. The assumption is that since a thing is past, it has no present meaning for us. But nothing could be further from the truth.

Whatever is still in memory is exactly what has most meaning for us. It is the indicator of the unfinished in life. It gives sure sign of what still has emotional significance for us. It refuses to allow us to overlook what must yet be acknowledged if we are ever to be fully honest with ourselves. Most of all, memory and the way we deal with it is the only thing we have that makes us authentic teachers of the young. It tells us what we did that now we miss doing, and it reminds us of what we didn't do that now we wish we had. And such things live in memory forever.

"I was young and my father was strict," the woman said. She was slim and chic, a very self-contained kind of person. "He wouldn't let me go to dances." She paused and looked away. "So, I left," she said. "I got on a train and went to California and I never came back home again." She paused again. "Until he died." And then the tears began to form. The sense of the old man's presence in that room hung there strong enough to taste. She was in her seventies, the wound still fresh.

Memory is many things. It is a call to resolve in us what simply will not go away. It is an invitation to delight in what is gone but is, too, the gold standard of our lives. It is a desire for completion, for continuance of something we once had but lost too soon. It is always an opportunity for healing. It preserves for us what must be faced and wrestled to the ground of the soul before the soul is free to fly. Without memory we could go blithely on in life without ever really knowing what of that life was still unfinished, was still rumbling around inside of us, waiting for attention.

Memory is the one function of the human mind that touches the core of us. It takes us back to where we came from, and it reminds us of what it was that drove us away as well. It is a clarion call to complete what was begun years ago, but has yet to be resolved in us. It tells us what we miss and what we regret and what we have yet to come to peace with, if our lives are ever to be really clear.

The wonder of being able to see life as a whole, at any time and all times, is the great gift of memory. It makes all of life a piece in progress. With one part of the soul in the past and another in the present, we are able to go on stitching together a life that has integrity and wholeness. Because of memory life is not simply one isolated act after another. It all fits into the image of the self and the goals of the heart. It makes them real. It makes them whole.

Memory holds us in contact with those who went before us. Sometimes it drenches us in the parts of the past we miss—and makes us sad. At other times, it leaves us wandering through the parts of life we did poorly and are sorry about still.

But memory is not meant to cement us in times past. It is

meant to enable us to do better now that which we did not do as well before. It is the greatest teacher of them all. The task is to come to the point where we can trust our memories to guide us out of the past into a better future.

There is nothing in conscious memory that is unimportant. To sit and listen to a person wander through the storied fragments of their lives is to come to know what worries them, what delights them, what love did to them, what rejection dampened in them, and what is left to deal with now if the press of past failures, the loss of past loves are ever to be stitched into a healthy whole in the here and now.

Memory allows for the ones we have treasured in life to live on inside of us, not in order to bind us to times past, but to remind us that life has been good before and can be just as good now.

And most of all, perhaps, memory also confronts us with the emotions—the feelings, the fears, the struggles—that reside in us yet as unfinished questions, as unresolved pain and unfinished joys. They tell us what is yet to be done. They become a blueprint for tomorrow that shows us out of our own experience how to live, how to love, how to forget, how to go on again.

Memories are not the shackles of the aging. On the contrary. They are the happy remembrance of possibilities still to be sought, or the now meaningful recall of things yet to be completed. They are the watermarks of our growth, the invitation to claim the joys of the past and the call to seek out those same things again, in different form, perhaps, but as promise of the same kinds of joy here and now.

A burden of memory in these years is to allow it to meld us into the company of people, time, and places long gone by.

A blessing of these years is to realize that our memories of both the sad and the happy, the exciting and the secure, the successes and the failures of life, are meant to guide us down these last roads with confidence—the confidence that having negotiated the demands of the past we may safely walk into the future.

FUTURE

"Old age," in Louis Kronenberger's view, "is an excellent time for outrage. My goal," he went on, "is to say or do at least one outrageous thing every week."

The "future," after seventy, is not a social boundary, a geographical place, a psychological presumption. It is a state of mind. One of two, in fact. We have all heard both of them expressed so often that we long ago stopped listening.

The one state of mind says, "We're all getting older. You just can't do those things anymore." The other says, "I've always wanted to see the Pyramids of Giza, so this year I'm going. I've always wanted to take mandolin lessons, so now I will."

The future is a very sweet part of getting older. It is something to be grasped with fervor. It gets more intense, more alive, more essential every day. To those who have finally become aware of the presence of time in their lives, the future is no longer "out there." The future is here, snapping at the heels, becoming more and more demanding as we go.

Most people live as if everything they are not doing now, they could simply do later. For them there is no urgency to life, just a long, quiet movement toward the acme of it. But not everyone.

Those who have come roaring into their sixties, full of life, relatively secure, brimming with ideas and finally full of self-confidence, come face-to-face with the meaning of mortality as they never have before. There is, they discover with a jolt, an end to time. Their time. The questions emerge then with fierce intensity: What is the purpose of time at this stage of my life where, it seems, being able to be interested in something has no purpose at all? Why this hiatus, this disconnect, between what I do and what I am? Everything worth doing seems to have run its course. The job is finished, the children are gone, life has gone stale, gone sour, gone cold. What do we do with time now? Do we simply live it out or fill it up? And if we're supposed to fill it up, with what and for what use?

The very thought of there being no work to get done, no deadlines to meet, no public demands to satisfy, no mountains left to climb offends everything these people felt was necessary to be alive.

Being edged off the upper shelf of life into a kind of shape-less, formless, substanceless nowhereland freezes their very souls. These are the ones who now keep reminding themselves and the rest of their world that "we're all getting older."

But there is another state of mind struggling to come alive now. There is the sense of urgency that comes with the aware-ness of time, the thought that there is so much else to life than what I have known till now. There is so much air out there that I have simply not allowed myself to breathe. There is the rest of life to be lived that I have been denied till now, ignored till now, been unaware of till now. Old age, like every other stage of life, is a learning time. It may be here, in fact, that we learn best what life is actually all about.

Old age is the time for letting out the spirit of outrage, the outrageous spirit that comes with having walked through the marketplace of life choosing between its fruits, looking for its pleasures, tasting and discarding as we go. Now, finally, we know what is missing, know what is good, know what is needed. Now we are beyond the narcissism of youth, above the survival struggles of young adulthood, beyond the grind of middle-age, and prepared to look beyond ourselves into the very heartbeat of life. Now we can let our spirits fly. We can do what our souls demand that fully human beings do. This is the moment for which we were born.

There is nothing to stop us now. Wherever we are needed, we can go now. Whatever we would like to do, we can do. Whatever must be said, we can say it. Mother Jones, nineteenth-century Irish immigrant to the United States, who worked in the sweatshops of New York for years, stood up in her sixties, organized the Knights of Labor, and led strikes and rallies for the welfare of the working class through her entire old age. "That woman," a congressman is said to have shouted in frustration, "is the most dangerous woman in America."

Old age is the time to be dangerous. Dangerously fun loving, dangerously honest. Dangerously involved. Dangerously alive. This is the time to go to Giza and to Washington, to parties and to political rallies, to music lessons, to the family that waits for us and to strangers who need us.

This is not the time to remember that "we are all getting older"—as if getting older were the curse of the damned. This is the time to do every single thing we can possibly do with all the life we can bring to it. This is the time to live with an edge, with strength, with abandon. There is nothing for which to save our energy. Now it is simply time to spend time well.

Is there a future for me when I get old? Indeed there is. The future at this stage in life is tomorrow.

Tomorrow is sacred. It is the great reminder of the gift of life. It is my whole resource. It is everything I have left to give. And it is not without purpose, whatever my situation, however differently I must go about it than I did twenty-five years ago. It is everything I have now with which to be the fullness of myself.

Most of all, tomorrow is for living, not for simply ambling around through life waiting to die. I will not be given tomorrow simply to allow myself to become one day older, one ounce less alive. Whatever I will do tomorrow will be sign to everyone around me that life is either to be lived to the brim, or wasted to go to dust, useless and desiccated years before its time. But that is to abandon those who look to me for wisdom, for purpose, and a glimpse of meaning for their own lives.

It is the elderly who are the real signs of what life has been about and is yet meant to be. To abandon such a responsibility smacks of the immoral. "To save one life," the rabbis say, "is to save the whole world." To save one life, as we get older, is to live our own life well.

A burden of these years is to assume that the future is already over.

A blessing of these years is to give another whole meaning to what it is to be alive, to be ourselves, to be full of life. Our own life.

AGELESSNESS

"The aging process," Doug Larson wrote, "has you firmly in its grasp if you never get the urge to throw snowballs."

Only children understand the impulsive, impetuous, impelling urge to throw snowballs. Only really wise adults realize that unless we throw them, it is unlikely we will ever manage to escape the traces that hold us down, hold us back, at any and every age. But that can only be learned from the young. And they can only learn from us when not to do it.

Getting in touch with the young again is what keeps us in touch with the world. And there are more ways to do it than we can imagine.

It's an odd sight, an old tire store, sitting there in a kind of stolid, institutional splendor in the midst of a street full of chopped-up old frame houses that rent or "board" three and four families at a time. It sits on the corner of the block, a showcase of sparkling gardens back and front. Framing the building on both sides of it in blazing color are life-size silhouettes of children. Here a child plays a piano, next to it a child in a tutu does a pirouette, along the back there is a paint palette, and beyond that a child on a stage. It is a living playhouse writ huge. There isn't a child in the world who wouldn't understand the signs and be drawn to them.

However rich and exciting this old refurbished auto repair building in the middle of the inner city, its name is unpretentious. "The Neighborhood Art House," it calls itself in large purple letters above the corner door. Every week over a hundred children, ages six to fourteen, run through the brick patio into the warren of practice rooms and art studios and writing corners and rows of computers they call their house. This is not school. There are no grades given here, no homework assignments, no punishments for doing what you like. They can play the drums there or practice ballet or read their poems or write their puppet shows or do an oil painting or two. And it's all for free, thanks to the people of the city. And that's impressive.

But just as impressive is to pass that corner in the summertime and see those children sitting bolt stark still on chairs on the patio, chin in hands, eyes wide open, as well-dressed men and women, all professionals of the city, past and present—lawyers, nurses, corporate types, retirees—sit in the sun and read to them aloud. The patio is filled with almost a hundred children per reading session, and the parking lot is filled with almost a hundred cars as adults scurry in and out, books under their arms.

Each child has a private reader who comes every day to do what no one does for these children otherwise: they read to them as if they were their own children, making animal sounds or changing voices from one character to another as they go. They fill their imaginations with leprechauns and the journeys of hot air balloons and the challenges faced by immigrant children and the wonders of the stars and the characteristics of dinosaurs.

More than that, they bridge the difference between childhood and parenthood for these children, between freedom and authority, the way grandparents were wont to do in decades past when children and grandparents lived in the same block, the same city, the same state. They fill children with a trust of adults. They open them to adult conversation, to adult influence. They give them a refuge from all the rules. They become friends, this child and that adult.

Intergenerational friendships between an older generation and a younger one are as important to the elder as they are to the child.

Children give us a lifeline to the present and the future that is denied to us if we sit alone in an independent-living unit. They don't play checkers much anymore, but they can teach us all about video games. They might not sing lullabies, but they know the words to every song on the radio. They tell us what the new language means. They keep us in touch with a warm and breathing world. They keep us warm and breathing, too.

Children release the child in us before it completely withers up and blows away. They connect us to the children of later generations in our own families, the ones we only see once a year or struggle to talk to on the phone.

They remind us that we are still part of the whole human race. We are not meant to be cordoned off from the rest of society. We are meant to be its wisdom center, its sign of a better life to come, its storehouse of the kind of lore no books talk about.

Once a society divides the human family as a matter of course, there is no family at all anymore. Instead, we have day care for children, senior citizen complexes for the elders, and condos where "families with children need not apply." We have a totally segregated and fractured society, with little or no way to grow through life together on a day-to-day basis. We have lost the right to learn from one another. Most of all, the older generation has been denied the right to teach. We are strangers to one another. We are out of touch with the fullness of the self.

This natural and necessary linkage between the old and the young cannot be reduced to a scheduled "activity for older citizens." This is the heartbeat of the culture we're talking about here. It keeps newness running in and out of our veins. It keeps ideas beyond murder, mayhem, drugs, and sex running in and out of theirs.

Relating to a child who is not theirs enables elders to reach out beyond themselves and the confines of their own private lives to become fully human again. And having elders who are not their parents take an interest in them, talk to them, show them things their parents do not have time to do—like how to fish, or how to fix a bike, or how to bake cookies, or how to pop corn the old fashioned way—enables the child to be anchored by an adult who is not also a disciplinarian.

A burden of these years is allowing ourselves to become isolated from the world around us.

A blessing of these years is finding a child who will help us to step out of all the old roles and become a human being again.

IMMEDIACY

"The secret of my vigor and activity," Lowell Thomas confessed, "is that I have managed to have a lot of fun."

There is a built-in danger in old age which, if we give in to it, makes aging one of the most difficult periods of life, rather than one of the most satisfying—which it should be. The danger of old age is that we may start acting old. And it is fun that keeps us laughing, and laughing that keeps us happy in the here and now. And it is in the here and now that we will spend the final stage of life, totally and only. But, oh, we get serious advice not to live fully and have fun.

"Act your age" can be useful advice when you're seventeen; it's a mistake when you're seventy-seven. When we start acting old, however old we are, we're finished. If we're really old when we start acting old, it's even worse. Then, acting our age is a terminal illness. We wear ourselves down to the point that we may be breathing but we are not living.

The fact is that there are no particular activities proper to being old in the same way that there are certain activities proper to all the other stages of life. It is proper between the ages of six and twenty-two to get an education. It is proper to have children and raise a family between twenty-two and fifty. It is proper to phase down a professional career sometime between sixty-five and seventy. But then, after that, the only thing that is peculiarly proper to getting older is whatever is going on at the moment.

If life is really for the living, then the trick to living well is to learn to live it fully, to soak it up, to revel in it.

What we too often fail to realize is that living fully depends a great deal more on our frame of mind, on our fundamental spirituality, than it does on our physical condition. If we see God as good, we see life as good. If we see God as a kind of sly and insidious Judge, tempting us with good things in order to see if we can be seduced into some sort of moral depravity by them, then life is a trap to be feared.

Living well has something to do with the spirituality of wholeheartedness, of seeing life more as a grace than as a penance, as time to be lived with eager expectation of its goodness, not in dread of its challenges. We are not given life in order to suffer. We are given life in order to learn to love the Creator through the joys and beauty of creation. We are given life in order to deal gracefully with the natural suffering of being mortal creatures.

When we fail to meet life head on, we fail to live it fully.

There are temptations for the elderly in the process that are particularly deluding because they sound so sensible while they are increasingly destructive.

"I'm too tired tonight. I don't think I'll go," we learn to say early in the aging process. But the others go on to the show or the party or the civic event, without us. "She's older now and can't do these things," they say. We teach them to ignore us and then wonder how it happened.

"That's too much effort. I don't do those things anymore," we say. So, we forgive ourselves the effort that comes with building the fire for the Fourth of July picnic. We don't do Christmas anymore. We don't send birthday cards. We do less and less all the time until sitting in place becomes the way we go through life.

"Oh, I've never done that before, and I'm not going to start now," we say. So we won't go to the concert in the park or learn to fish or call donors for the parish bazaar. We drop out of living just as surely as if we were already gone and buried. And we do it to ourselves.

"Get in that thing just to see a waterfall?" we say. "Not I! That's downright dangerous." So, we never get to see the mist from Niagara Falls. We won't admire the Rockies from a mountaintop observatory. We don't look out over Puget Sound from the Space Needle in Seattle. We don't feel. We deny ourselves layer upon layer of life and wonder why life holds no excitement for us anymore.

"Go away for a weekend?" we say.

"Take a continuing education course?" we argue.

"Do you know how much that costs?" we insist.

"Buy a computer just to send e-mails?" we question.

"Stay away an extra couple of days? What will happen to the plants?" we wonder.

So we don't go the next step to begin something new. We fail to go on becoming. We stop in our tracks with years ahead of us. And wait. We take the gift of life and return it unopened.

"Well, that sounds like a nice thing to do, but I don't have anyone to take along," we say. So, instead of reaching out to make new friends and find other companions and join different groups, we dig our holes and pull them in after us.

"I'm past those things," we argue, as if life were a series of graded exercises, open to some but not to others. We're past doing a carnival ride with the children. We're past going out on New Year's Eve. We're past reading a book on the beach. We simply burrow into our nests and let life go by.

But if we do that we let the chance to meet people go by with it. And have experiences. And find the growth within that is yet to be tapped, as well.

Life is not simply what happens to us—though in moments of surprise life waits, too—but life is also what we ourselves make happen.

We become what we do. We become new inside when we urge ourselves to do new things. We become awake when we do not allow ourselves to simply sleep through life. We become more sure of ourselves when we forget our age and trust ourselves enough to refuse to fear everything in life from a pair of stairs to a mountain incline.

We aren't "past" life unless we allow life to pass us by.

No, we can't do everything. Yes, we may well get tired more easily, get exhausted more quickly. There are, of course, some things that would require so much effort that we should rather be doing more enjoyable, less physically strenuous things. Certainly, many of the old friends with whom years of companionship made us real comfortable are gone. And some things are indeed beyond our budgets. But none of those circumstances justify our substituting breath for life.

It is time now to begin again, to become new, to find ways to enjoy life, to seize every opportunity to be an exciting, interesting, significant person. We owe the world the best of ourselves because all the rest of the world is struggling with something, too.

A burden of these years is that we might allow ourselves to become less than what we are able to be more quickly than we ever should.

A blessing of these years is that they call us to go down deep into ourselves in order to discover everything we are. Now. Right now.

NOSTALGIA

"I have no romantic feelings about age," Katharine Hepburn once said. "Either you are interesting at any age or you are not. There is nothing particularly interesting about being old—or being young, for that matter."

Indeed, the truth is that there is no perfect, no ultimate, no crowning stage of life. Whatever we are now, that is it. If we privilege one stage of life over the others, we stand to miss their pulp.

Yes, it's good to think back, to remember the people who prodded us to begin the great projects of life, who pushed us to go on when quitting would have been easier—but it can also be destructive in the long run. It's good to know where we've come from so that we can measure the distance from here to where we're going. It's good to remember all the joys of life so that in dark times we can have the confidence that the good times will come back—because they always have.

But it is not good to make the past the acme of our lives. It is not good to make youth the shrine at which we worship once we have moved into another stage of life. It is not good to resist becoming what we are and wishing instead to be what we are not.

The temptation, far too often, far too common, is to try to freeze life in place, to become fixated in one phase of it or another, to fail to move beyond the moment.

One of the clearest signs of the way different people view life lies in the way they deal with the death of those dear to them. For some it is the day life stops moving. They stop in their tracks, paralyzed with pain, steeped in loss. For others it is a crossover moment in time. These people face the pain and set about to move with it but beyond it. We've all seen both approaches to the end of one phase of life, the beginning of another one, but it can take a while before we understand the implications of what we're seeing.

The day after the funeral a few friends stopped by to see how the widow was doing. The crowds would be gone by then. The emptiness would surely start. No one to talk to about it. No one to reminisce with over lunch. No one to distract her from the heaviness of the day. She would need someone there.

All things considered, the death had been sudden. There was no long illness during which to come to grips with the eventual loss. There was the accident, the infection, the trips to the hospital, the coma, the long, silent going. The pain would all come now.

She was in the back of the house when they got there. "Can you bring another couple of those large boxes in with you as you come?" she called. Three or four of the boxes were already full, taped shut and stacked by the kitchen door.

In the bedroom, she was bent over the dresser drawers, rummaging through clothes. Men's shirts were stacked on one side of the bed, suits and ties on the other. "Oh, good," she said when she saw the boxes. "Now I can get these things packed up, too."

The shelves and dresser tops had been stripped clean. The door to the empty cupboard stood idly open. Everything else in the room, apparently, had already been bundled up and boxed. Then, as if in answer to the unspoken question, she said, "Life goes on, you know. We cannot make the present a shrine to the past."

Indeed, life does go on. We cannot arrest it. We must not arrest it. It is not possible to live in the past, however much the temptation to try. If life is for the living and we do not live it, we doom ourselves to premature death. What's even more pathetic, we do it in the name of the very relationships and places and events that brought us to growth in years gone by. These very seedbeds enable us to trust that new growth will come out of the darkness within us now.

There is a thin line between memory and nostalgia. They are not the same thing.

Memory is recollection. Good memories make us laugh on gray days and bring us old warmth on cold nights. They gather around us all the ghosts of yesterday we need to urge us on. They enable us to have faith in the future because they remind us that the past has been so life-giving, so full of hope in all the tomorrows of life. Memories are treasure-houses of warnings and of trust, of productive pain and precious goadings. Memories do not so much immerse us in the past as they prod us toward the future.

Nostalgia is something different entirely. Nostalgia is not simply recollection of the past. Nostalgia is immersion in the past. Nostalgia traps us, one foot in the present, one foot in the yesterday. But the melancholy of nostalgia is *not* the geography of old age. Possibility is.

Every stage of life is interesting if we will only allow ourselves to explore all its delights. Old age is the most interesting of them all. Now we are the shapers of our own destiny, the makers of our own delights, the custodians of our own personality. What we talk about now, what we do now, what we become now is entirely our own responsibility. To encase it all in the past, when we were unfinished, when we were still at the mercy of circumstances far outside our control, is to trifle with the sweetest time of life.

Nostalgia is a dangerous temptation to confuse love for part of life with love for all of life. It substitutes the delight of the present for the fantasies of the past.

Nostalgia is not memory. Nostalgia is pining and yearning and longing for what was good for us in the past, but which would be totally out of kilter with the here and now.

The seduction latent in nostalgia is the temptation to take refuge in what is no more, rather than to face the exigencies of the present with good humor and brave hearts. It is a snapshot of the past, edited to suit us. We remember the days on the old boat, but conveniently forget the trouble of cleaning and hauling and rowing the thing. We remember the beloved dog, but forget the barking and the jumping and the damage it did to the couch. Unless we can deal with both dimensions of every aspect in life, we begin to use memory to escape both the reality of the present and the reality of the past as well.

It is a beguilingly dangerous temptation of old age, this return to an unreal past. It is an easy trap for those who are tired of living, tired of adjusting, tired of keeping up with life. And so, ironically, it tends to exaggerate the life they had and destroy the life they have. It affects the way we look at life now. It shapes what we talk about. It makes us interesting for awhile, maybe, our stories and all their charm—but then it makes us not interesting at all. People tire quickly of conversations that are simply ongoing narratives, endlessly repeated narratives, of another time. They do not look to the older generation for nostalgia. They look to us for wisdom, for courage, for proof that life in all its forms is not only possible but wonderful.

The burden of nostalgia is that it takes us out of the present and immobilizes us in the past.

The blessing of nostalgia is that it can serve to remind us that just as we survived all of life before this, grew from it, laughed through it, learned from it as well, we can also live through this age with the same grace, the same insights—and this time, share that audacious spirit with others.

SPIRITUALITY

"Age puzzles me," wrote Florida Scott-Maxwell, the Jungian psychologist, in her journal, *The Measure of My Days*, which she kept in her eighties. "I thought it was a quiet time. My seventies were interesting and fairly serene but my eighties are passionate. I grow more intense as I age."

And why not? If, as the years go by, we grow more and more aware of both the meaning and the meaninglessness of things, we must certainly also grow more sensitive, not less aware, of the ebb and flow of life. We do not simply ignore life as we get older, but we do engage with it at a different level, out of different motives, with a more focused heart.

If we learn anything at all as time goes by and the changing seasons become fewer and fewer, it is that there are some things in life that cannot be fixed. It is more than possible that we will go to our graves with a great deal of personal concerns, of life agendas, left unresolved. That becomes clearer and clearer by the year. Some of the family fractures will not yet have healed. Some of the words spoken in heat and haste will not have been redeemed. Some of the friendships will not have been renewed. Some of the dreams will never be realized. So has life been wasted? Has it all been for nothing?

Only if we mistake the meaning of the last period of life. This time of life is not meant to solidify us in our inadequacies. It is meant to free us to mature even more.

To hope that in the end all the ruptures will have been repaired, however, is at best unreal. People are long gone and even longer out of touch. Nothing can be done at this late stage to reopen the conversations, let alone fix the rifts or heal the lingering wounds.

Many of the things for which we still feel responsible, even feel guilty about, we couldn't do anything to undo now—even if we wish we could. We can't put back together a failed marriage. We can't cancel the years of neglect, a lifetime of indifference, a history of disregard for the people who had a right to expect our concern. There is nothing we can do now about a lifetime of lack of contact with our children, the tension we felt with our mother, the distance we felt from our father, the jealousies and outbursts and petty irritations that marked years long past, that call up still all our own defenses. That time, those situations, are simply gone. Out of our hands. Beyond our control.

Inside the scars still smart, though. We have been hurt. We have done the hurting. We made the mistakes. We created the mess that came from them. And there is not now and never was, as far as we could see, any way to put Humpty-Dumpty back together again. So now what?

If we cannot deal directly with all the unfinished struggles of our lives, how can we possibly face the end of life with any kind of serenity?

The fact is that the unrest that accumulates over the years is the very grace reserved for the end time, the last years, the pinnacle of life. Only now can the consciousness of these wrongs really make a difference in us. Only now can this pain be made productive. Why? Because now we must deal with it all ourselves. There is no one here to forgive us anymore, no one to tell us we were right, no one to surrender to our insistence, no one left for us to refuse to consort with. Instead, it is all alive within us. Now we must go down into the deepest part of ourselves and come to peace, not with our old antagonists but, more importantly than that, with ourselves, with the conscience we have been refusing to reconcile with for years.

There are issues far more germane to what happened in our life than simply the questions of who did what to whom and why and what happened to us as a result. Instead, what must be addressed now is what we became as a result of them. Did we become a fuller human being—or did we only go through life proclaiming our innocence despite the soul song within that told us how guilty we really were?

This is the period of life when we must begin to look inside our own hearts and souls rather than outside ourselves for the answers to our problems, for the fixing of the problems. This is the time for facing ourselves, for bringing ourselves into the light.

This is the period of spiritual reflection, of spiritual renewal in life. Now is the time to ask ourselves what kind of person we have been becoming all these years. And do we like that person? Did we become more honest, more decent, more caring, more merciful as we went along because of all these things? And if not, what must we be doing about it now?

Whatever caused the rifts in our life, we had some part in the making of them. What of that demanding, narcissistic, spoiled child yet remains in us? And are we willing now to deal with the dross of it?

As the body begins to go to air, as we begin to melt into the beyond, are we able to put down those things in us that have been an obstacle between us and the rest of creation all our lives?

Can we come eye to eye with our own souls and admit who we are? If we have been selfish, can we bring ourselves to the daily discipline of caring for others? If we have been dishonest about ourselves, can we take care now to tell the real truth about ourselves? If we have been God-less, are we able to trust that the Creator of Life must therefore also be the home of our souls, and can we bow before the Life that has claim on our own?

Can we begin to see ourselves as only part of the universe, just a fragment of it, not its center? Can we give ourselves to accepting the heat and the rain, the pain and the limitations, the inconveniences and discomforts of life, without setting out to passively punish the rest of the human race for the daily exigencies that come with being human?

Can we smile at what we have not smiled at for years? Can we give ourselves away to those who need us? Can we speak our truth without needing to be right and accept the vagaries of life now—without needing the entire rest of the world to swaddle us beyond any human justification for expecting it? Can we talk to people decently and allow them to talk to us?

Old people, we're told, become more difficult as they get older. No. Not at all. They simply become less interested in maintaining their masks, more likely to accept the effort of being human, human beings. They no longer pretend. They face the fact that now, this period, this aging process, is the last time we're given to be more than all the small things we have allowed ourselves to be over the years. But first, we must face what the smallness is, and rejoice in the time we have left to turn sweet instead of more sour than ever.

A burden of these years is the danger of giving in to our most selfish selves.

A blessing of these years is the opportunity to face what it is in us that has been enslaving us, and to let our spirit fly free of whatever has been tying it to the Earth all these years.

LONELINESS

"What is the worst of woes that wait on age?" Lord Byron wrote. "What stamps the wrinkle on the brow? To view each loved one blotted from life's page and be alone on earth as I am now."

One of the major characteristics of the aging process is that it separates us from the rest of humanity. The older we get, the younger the rest of the world appears to us, the more we are aware that we now inhabit a very rare space. As family patriarchs disappear around us, as friends go the way of the last amen, we begin to realize that we are more and more alone. There are fewer now who understand who we are, where we've been, what we care about in life. Their lives are very different. They do not know our losses.

Age is the elegy of elegies. It has a greater impact than death in many ways. In death you are remembered. In age, you are far more likely to feel forgotten, sequestered even from the very act of living.

"Uncle Otto," the child said loudly, "you're the oldest one in the whole family now." The room, it seemed, got a little quieter. A kind of uneasy knowledge hung over the group. David, clearly, had spoken the unspeakable.

David was nine. The unspeakable meant nothing to him. Uncle Otto was ninety. The unspeakable, the awareness that if people die in rank, the oldest member of the family might well be the next to go, meant everything to him. This family gathering could very well be the last one he, too, would ever attend again. It was Christmastime, after all, and the family was keenly aware that Aunt Annie, who had been ninety the Christmas before, was no longer with them.

Otto sat very still, very upright, smartly dressed, alert—even handsome in a way. He was a small man but a wiry one with a clear eye, a straight back, and a steady step. He was not "ninety"; he was Uncle Otto. If people were waiting for a discussion of what it feels like to be ninety years old, they were not going to get it from him.

And that is most proper. The question is really not Uncle Otto's question at all. It is a question for all of us once we discover that we are the oldest person in almost every gathering we go into. We are the ones who have to answer ourselves every day, "How does it feel to live in a younger world while being so old?"

There is a loneliness that seeps in as we age. It is the loneliness that distances ourselves from where we've come from and to where we're going. We begin to be less and less here and more and more . . . where? It is the preoccupation with the where-ness that begins to take over.

On the one hand, we're lonely, even in a crowd, because there are so few, if any, we can talk to about this new moment in our lives. And on the other hand, it does not feel real, even to us.

Age, we know, is nothing but a number. Except that it isn't.

Things begin to happen to us that make the number real. We begin to be aware that life is slipping between our fingers like the oil of fine olives, smoothly and steadily, smoothly and regularly, smoothly but inevitably.

That's when we get lonely, not because we are being isolated or ignored, but precisely because we are now in the fullness of life. Our own. We are not living the life of the masses anymore. And our life, we have come to understand, is very different from theirs.

We miss the sense of importance that came with the bustle of middle age. At least we miss it until we become conscious of the new importance that comes with simply being who we are, rather than simply what we did. Until that time arrives, there is the feeling that we are all talking to one another under water: we do not really know what they are talking about anymore. And that is very frightening. And the people around us, people we've known a long time, do not understand us either. We do not tell them either the fear or the pain that goes with finding ourselves now in a world of our own, with nothing to say that they could possibly understand or begin to be interested in.

We miss the daily social stimulation that came with going into the office, the shop, the store, the classroom, the hospital, and being a part of the team, the crowd, the birthday parties, the neighborhood barbecues. Even if there are lots of people around, they are people we've never really been with before, and we don't really know any of them. Recognize them maybe, speak to them maybe, but not really know them as we knew the longtime companions of our lives.

We miss the intellectual stimulation, sense of achievement,

of being needed, that came with the daily problems. We miss being part of the work, the project, the goal, the great glorious accomplishments that no one ever heard about but us.

We miss having a place to fill.

There was a time when older people stayed in the family all their lives. At one time, you didn't retire till you retired—or, more likely, not at all. Before all these changes, we were people, not retirement dates.

True. All true. On the other hand, there was no television to keep older people informed back then. There was no Internet to keep them in touch with their far-flung family and friends. There was no way to become part of something even bigger and more important than the work they did, once the work was over. Now, people look for people who will take the time to do what society really needs to have done. They look for people who are involved in something because it is worth doing, not because it pays well.

Then we discover that if we're lonely, it may be because we have not looked around to see who needs us.

A person who is needed—really needed—is never lonely, never isolated, never without purpose in life. All we need to do is to go out and do something. The world is waiting for us with open arms.

A burden of these years is that we will hole up somewhere and mourn our age, our change in life, our losses.

A blessing of these years is that we will make ourselves available to the world that is waiting for us, even now, even here.

FORGIVENESS

"The young know the rules," Oliver Wendell Holmes wrote. "The old know the exceptions."

There is a softening of heart that comes with age, not out of virtue so much as out of experience. By seventy, we not only know that no one is perfect, we know that no one can be. Not we, not they, not anybody. In fact, we learn as the years go by that life is nothing but a series of exceptions to be reckoned with, to be mediated, to be understood. Our standards are only that—standards. They are not absolutes, and those who seek to make them so soon fall in the face of their own rigidities.

We know these things now with the kind of knowledge that can only come from knowing ourselves, from the awareness of our own failings, our own mistakes, our great desire to be perfect and, whatever our efforts at anything, our own cavernous need for mercy. We know this and a great many other things as well now, all of them to be reckoned with more kindly, more lovingly, more softly. The problem is that once we know something, we can never not know it. It requires a new kind of honesty from us. It burdens us with its truth.

Age is a veritable mineshaft of hard-won truths. Marriage is not a matter of always and only "living happily ever after," we discover. Youth is not "carefree," no matter who says so. Governments are not unfailingly worth our "allegiance," and religions, too, "sin," we learn. But maybe more compelling than any other is the awareness that having been failed against, we too have failed. We not only have much to forgive, we have much to be forgiven for—if not by others, at least by ourselves. Alfred Lord Tennyson put it this way: "Two aged men, that had been foes for life, Met by a grave, and wept—and in those tears They washed away the memory of their strife; Then wept again the loss of all those years."

It is often not so much what we have done or what has been done to us, but what we have done because of it that is the greater grief. Family feuds go on for generations, for instance, far beyond the time when anybody remembers, if they ever knew, exactly how the rift started or why. Worse still than breaches of the family are the friendships that collapse and the time that is lost between us because, unlike the family, there are no natural meeting points to bring two people back together again. Even if against our will.

Too often, in the passion of the moment, young and full of the venom of perfectionism, we demand our due. And when it does not come, we stomp testily away, righteous in our anger, martyred in our souls. Better to be a victim than a loser. We have been wronged. Someone has broken the unwritten rules of life by which we live. Someone has scratched the surface of our own perfection and left us exposed, abandoned, distant, aloof, gone. Sometimes the other person knows what happened, and why. Sometimes he or she doesn't. We simply disappear to wait for a redress that never comes.

Then, the years pass. The more important the relationship, the more vivid the memory of the wrong. Instead of diminishing, the memory—the pain of it—grows stronger every year. This is a weeping wound, festering with time, a scar on the heart, acid in the belly. And time is passing.

Only forgiveness can stem such pain in us. An apology alone can't possibly do it. This kind of pain, held to the breast all these years, licked and nurtured, fed by time and polished by the ages, can be healed only by the wounded, not the offender, because it is the wounded who is maintaining it.

The hardness is in my heart now. It is far and beyond the hard-heartedness of the one who plunged the knife. It is mine. I own it. I fostered it. And I am suffering from it more than the person I hold responsible for the hurt.

Such is the unfinished business of relationship. The question is, why does such an old sore hurt more now that I am old than it did when it happened? Or, conversely, why am I more sensitive to it now than I have been for years? And the answer is, "because." Because I am older now. Because I feel the rush of time now. Because I see my own foolishness now. Because I realize that the distance this has put between me and someone I loved has been much more damaging to my soul than the offense could possibly have been. Because I have finally learned over time that the rules are not nearly so important in life as the exceptions to them. Because too many years of life have been wasted on what is not worth a life already. Because it is time to value exception more than recrimination.

Recrimination never really solves anything. It only evens the scales. It does not turn the need for justice into the balm of love. It does not give me back to myself, a little more humble, perhaps, and a great deal more human as well. Only forgiveness can do that.

Only forgiveness is the therapy of old age that wipes the slate clean, that heals as it embraces.

The unselfish generosity of forgiveness is a myth. Forgiveness is more important to the one who forgives than it is to the one who is forgiven.

Bitterness, once it sinks like sand in the soul, skews our balance for years to come. It is always there, scratching and digging and eating and burning the heart out of us. We smile at some, of course, but the smile is more pretense than real. We are not really open, not really loving, not really a happy person. And the end of time draws nearer.

Only we can free ourselves from the burden of bitterness old anger brings with it still. Only we can begin to look for the exceptions that make this a forgivable offense rather than immutable malevolence. Do we even remember clearly anymore what it was that happened? Are we really sure it was as intentional as we have painted it all these years? Is there nothing that explains it, that mitigates it, that makes it understandable? "Is there anyone we wouldn't love," poet Mary Lou Kownacki writes, "if we only knew their story?"

Hasn't too much time been wasted on this little bit of nothingness already? Is this the kind of thing we want to have continue to weigh us down as we spend the last of our days, the best of our days? Is this the shrunken end to which we have brought ourselves? Is this the distance we want between us and life, now that we know how wonderful life is really meant to be?

Forgiveness puts life back together again. It is proof of our own learnings. It is sign of our own inner healing. It is mark of our own self-knowledge. It is the measure of the divine in us.

Old age tells us that we ourselves have failed often, have never really done anything completely right, have never truly been perfect—and that that is completely all right. We are who we are—and so is everyone else. And it is our forgiveness of others that gains for us the right to forgive ourselves for being less than we always wanted to be.

A burden of these years is that we run the risk of allowing ourselves to be choked by the struggles of the past.

A blessing of these years is the ability to see that life does not have to be perfect to be perfect; it only needs to be forgiving—and forgiven.

OUTREACH

"Few persons," La Rochefoucauld wrote, "know how to be old."

Indeed, it takes a lot of learning. Being young in this society is easy. It has all the magnetism of the Holy Grail. Youth is what this world is about. Hardly an ad does not extol it. Medicines promise it. Conditioning programs guarantee it. Being young, we are made to believe, is the real definition of life. And in one sense, that's true.

The tenor of a youthful society, however, with its speed and noise and energy, its push and drive and certainty, rather than bringing hope, is, at the same time, all too often very isolating. Everyone else is young. But I am not. So what is left for me now when push and drive seem no longer to be the elixir of life?

Age, in a youth-oriented culture, can become a very depressing thing. Writers over the age of thirty in Hollywood, they tell us, face dour prospects. Producers fear that the over-thirty crowd, however talented they may be, are now too out of touch to be able to communicate with a younger crowd. And that is essential because this age cohort, they call them, is the largest-growing economic segment of society. The advertising industry knows how important that is. And we are made to know that, too. That age group drives this society.

It's a stifling thought.

A culture built on creating needs in children and then catering to them bodes little good for the age to come. It leaves an older generation at the mercy of a world whose agendas are now totally out of touch with their own. Worse, it threatens to create in society at large a video-game mentality where fast is better than slow, young is better than old, and violence is an easy answer to everything. Video-game victims do not bleed; they do not suffer; they simply burst in midair. Forget slow and thoughtful approaches to serious issues. Forget the accumulation of knowledge that accrues over time. Forget reason and education, age and wisdom, where violence will do.

Silently but steadily, that kind of culture and environment isolates an older population on an island of its own. A basically invisible one. A very sparsely nurtured one. And the older people themselves, with their predilection for talk and thought and analysis, like digitized targets on a game console, simply vanish off the production charts. Of the over 150 television channels available, for instance, only a handful play classical music, televise book discussions, schedule debates on national issues, or produce programs on drama and art. Whatever reflection material a society needs to enable it to judge this year's political, social, or economic issues against a thousand years of earlier thought on similar subjects has been squeezed dry of it.

No one senses the dearth of it more than the growing population of elderly. Those who do not articulate the impact and prevalence of ageism nevertheless come to suffer from the isolating effects of it. People living alone in this society increased from 17 percent of all households in 1970 to 26 percent of housing units in 2000.[23] Whole villages of older women and men have sprung up, segregated from the larger population around them. And so, sadly, they lose contact, lose energy, and lose respect just when they know more now about living than they ever did before.

What's worse, tragic stories of what is happening to the isolated elderly now come from all over the world—from Australia and France, from Germany and from the United States. They live in apartments for the elderly, they stay in their own homes, they live in public housing, they live in expensive condos. But while these elderly come from all levels and sectors of society, all kinds of cities, all manner of busy and populated neighborhoods, their stories share a common end: they all die alone and no one discovers them for days, or weeks, or even for months.

The explanations range from lack of city services to the need for electronic monitoring aids, from negligent families to lack of "community spirit." How is it, people ask, that someone can die and their absence not be noted, not be attended to, not be signaled in any way whatsoever? Indeed, big cities can be the most anonymous, most reclusive places in the world. And so can we.

In a mobile society, families are spread across the country. No one is just dropping in to see grandma anymore. People work different places now and are more inclined to socialize with coworkers than with neighbors. Social groups form outside the neighborhood now—in bowling alleys or at company events, in civic groups or private clubs, in parish activities or in special-interest groups. We don't know who's in the building anymore, let alone who's on the block.

No doubt about it, city life does not function on the model of the rural village or the small-town community. We are a world of strangers trying to find space in overcrowded areas to be alone, to be individuals, to have privacy.

Most of the time, we get personal privacy in this day and age by creating psychological distance where we don't have physical space. We don't talk on elevators. We don't sit on porches anymore. We don't walk the street at night greeting people from doorstep to doorstep. We don't know the pharmacist or the mail carrier or the banker by name—and they don't know us. Clearly, the whole world has to learn anew how to relate to the people next door if we are ever to be a genuine community, a civilized world again. Otherwise, no wonder people can be dead for days and never be missed.

But part of the problem is also that, too often, the older we get, the less we ourselves keep contact with the world around us. We call no one, write to no one, socialize with no one. As if there were no place for us in life, no one who needs us, no one who waits for our call as much as we wait for theirs.

There is then another reality to be reckoned with when we bemoan the isolation that so often comes as we get older. It is ourselves. The fact is that we don't have to be isolated if we don't isolate ourselves. Outreach is at the kernel of getting older. We need to go out to meet the rest of the world, rather than wait for the world to come to us.

The hall was full to overflowing, for instance, when Helen and Herman retired. This was clearly not an isolated couple.

They were well into their eighties, but they were known by everybody in the city, sought after by every organization in town. For years, Helen and Herman had run the local soup kitchen single-handedly on Mondays. She did the cooking, organized the other volunteers, dished up food and called every visitor in the food line by name, then Herman cleaned and locked up when the supper hour was over. She had cancer, bad legs, and a series of chronic diseases. They never kept her from going to the kitchen till she finally succumbed to family pressure and left Mondays to someone else.

What does it take to be loved as much as Helen and Herman as you get older?

How is it that some elderly simply fit in and take over—and others die alone and unmissed for months?

Generativity—the act of giving ourselves to the needs of the rest of the world—is the single most important function of old age. For example, in all three social strata of George Vaillant's Harvard Study of Adult Development—Harvard men, inner-city men, and college women—it was widening their social circle as life went on that was the key factor in the achievement of successful aging, not money, not education, not family.[24]

But this "widening" was not simply the creation of social contacts, as important as that is. Instead these individuals created social contacts by doing more than that—they became actively involved in one or more of the great social activities of life, "helping someone else."

In fact, most of the important dimensions of public life depend on the volunteer services of older people. They do the caretaking of other elderly, they supervise the children of young parents too busy now to do it all themselves. They prepare and deliver the "Meals on Wheels" that enable so many older people to remain in their own homes. They prepare the civic posters and the election ballots. They volunteer in libraries and museums and in hospitals and parks. They do the research now which they could not do while they were teaching. They write the books they did not have time to outline while they worked. They create the discussion groups, the reading groups, the study groups, the social events that make the world go round. "If you want to know if your work in life is over and you're still alive," the Sufi master says, "it isn't."

They are the givers of the world, and with their giving comes a wide network of contacts, of friends, of people who depend on them, need them, look to them for answers.

Most important of all, perhaps, is that old age is the only age when we can possibly be so important to the world at large because it is the first time in life when we ourselves are free enough to give much thought to a world broader than our own. We are ready now to stretch ourselves beyond ourselves for the sake of all the others to whom we are leaving this world.

A burden of these years is the danger of considering ourselves useless simply because we are no longer fulfilling the roles and positions of youth.

A blessing of these years is the freedom to reach out to others, to do everything we can with everything in life that we have managed to develop all these years in both soul and mind for the sake of the rest of the human race.

THE PRESENT

"Nothing is inherently and invincibly young except spirit," George Santayana said. "And spirit can enter a human being perhaps better in the quiet of old age and swell there more undisturbed than in the turmoil of adventure."

One of the most obvious lifestyle changes, after the long years of family and work routine end, is the change in the nature of our days. Life takes on a different pace now, one that is not always a comfortable one. It doesn't take long before we begin to suffer from what we thought would be one of the greatest joys of age, the reckless sense of abandon that comes from having time on our hands. The problem is that reckless as we might be, we simply don't know what to do when there is nothing "to do."

One of the results of having lived a regime of regularly scheduled days for almost our entire life is that we can easily lose the spirit of play. Not only do our bodies age, but our spirits can mildew a bit, too. Whether we know it or not, life has lost some of its sense of possibility, of abandon, over the years.

More importantly, the sense of play, the quality in us that really keeps us young, after years of having been largely ignored, has been sapped of its electric edge. It may even take a while to retrieve it. But retrieve it we must if we are to let age have free rein in us.

Age is meant for the revival of the spirit. Age is meant to allow us to play—with ideas, with projects, with friends, with life.

One of the better gifts of growing older is that time becomes more meaningful. Time now becomes a companion on the way. We are aware of it always, hovering over us like a chilling mist, a warming sun—waking us to the power of the immediate.

Moments are not lived casually once we approach old age. Now, they are savored. Every layer of them is milked, wrung out, and relished. Never has the present had more spice. Never has every day been more delicious, more painful, more liberating, more worrisome, more completely drained of every minute in it than when we begin to count the ones that may be left to us. Never have our spirits been more alive.

There actually is no time to waste anymore. The now is no longer one moment on the way to another one. It is everything there is to life.

When we learn to sink into the moment with that much passion, that much pure, unadulterated sensuousness, we finally learn to be alive.

All the rest of life has been for the sake of coming to this time in it. Everything else has been pure practice for this time, simply gestures of what it is to live fully.

It is only in the present that we learn to live, and it is the present that is the focus of old age. We live here now, only here—and oh, so deliberately so.

Things we never saw, never really saw, before this time—things we owned and held and had seen all our lives—abruptly, almost for the first time, become glaringly present. We begin to realize the way babies smile back if we smile at them long enough. We begin to wonder how it is that in a still sea, the water continues to lap at the beach. We understand that the pain in a loved one's eye must be addressed now, before it becomes too late to staunch it.

The present finds its way into the center of our souls as it has never done before.

Appreciation becomes acute as time goes by. We come to understand that the sensibility of appreciation flowers best in the heightened awareness of the present that comes with age. We begin to smell smells we never paid attention to before, because we were too busy with paperwork and tools and shopping or the weight of a basket of wash waiting to be done. Now we find it so easy just to sit outside a bakery to smell the fresh bread. With the smell comes the past, of course, but with it comes a sense of loveliness about the present, as well. All of life has not deserted us. In fact, maybe we have never in our lives known so much real life before this. Now we can sit with it, see its implications, become intoxicated with its meaning.

But the present is more than appreciation. It is urgency, the kind that drives us to do more than we ever thought we could do in a single day. Most people, we come to realize, stand at the lathe all day, or sit at the desk all day, or run after the children all day, or race through traffic all day, or stare at a clock all day. Not us. Not the young-old or the old-old. We go from place to place because we want to be there; because we are happy to be able to be there; because we know that being there is gift and grace to us, not hardship, not boredom, not waste. We go through time leaving our mark on it for the sake of times to come.

We become attuned in a different way to the marks of those who have gone before us as well. Who made that old bench in the park, we wonder. And, in our hearts, we thank the ones who carried the stone, the ones who engraved it, the ones who cemented it down so that it would be safer for the likes of us. So that it will be there for years to come.

Indeed, we say to ourselves, no one lives for nothing. But, we realize with a kind of pang, we never thought that before this moment. Ah, age . . .

The present, always a kind of revolving door of life taking us from one thing to the other, is now exactly what slows us down. It stops us because we have come to realize, in the strongest kind of way, maybe, that we have a past—that point of discontinuity in our own lives where what we thought would always be, disappeared. And, if truth were told, the power of the present lies in making us aware that there may not be much of a future left. Ten years, hopefully. Five, surely. Tomorrow, God willing.

It is the present, then, that reminds us constantly of the value of the obvious. We may not pass this way again. After this trip, how many more will there be? But then, who cares? This one has been so good. This one has been so beautiful. Does it really matter how many more there are? The only reason anyone ever needs to repeat anything is so that they can finally come to experience it fully.

The present of old age, the age we bring to the present, unveils to us the invisibility of meaning. Everything in life is meaningful—once we come to see it, to experience it, to look for it. Once we really come into the fullness of the present. Then we cease to take life for granted.

Life is now. Only now. But who of us has ever much stopped to notice it? We did what we did in all those other years because those were the tasks of life then. But the task of life now is, simply, life. What we haven't lived till now is waiting for us still. Behind every moment the spirit of life, the God of life, waits. Every small thing we do is meant to take us deeper into its substance. "In this," the mystic Julian of Norwich said, holding an acorn, "is everything that ever was." And she was right. In that tiny burst of life were all the elements of all the life in the world. In this moment, in the now of life, is everything we have ever been and will become. And it is calling us, now, to be that to its fullness, and even more.

The present is what takes us into the center of ourselves, asking us, where have you been all this time? How did you miss that, forget this, overlook what has always been behind this moment? When you raced to work, did you understand that work was about being cocreative in this world? When you made love, did you realize that love was about the ecstasy of the divine in life? When you were hurt and rejected and left out, did you know that being left out of someone else's circle was meant simply to bring you to realize the value and the strength of the self?

The present is the friend of age, not its enemy. It inundates us with life. It soaks us in the brine of it. It gives us the space and time to realize that without the past, we could not possibly live this present so well.

The burden of the present is that it brings us to face the fleetingness of time.

The blessing of the present is that it brings us to understand the fleetingness of time—to live with the spirit in full bloom.

APPRECIATION

"How beautiful the leaves grow old," John Burroughs wrote. "How full of light and color are their last days."

When there is little else in life to do but live well, life itself becomes all the more precious, all the more striking in its many layers of beauty. Shells on the beach become artifacts fit for keeping. Wind on a dry day becomes a new insight into the glare of creation. Someone else's smile bonds us to the entire human community. The problem may simply be that we take so long to be shocked by the power of normalcy. We see, but only lately. We hear the world around us, but only partially. We sense the symphony of life, but only weakly. And then, suddenly, when there is nothing between us and the raw, tart, sweet center of life to obscure it, there it is, alive and glowing right before our eyes.

Appreciation becomes us, but too often comes late.

In a restaurant sat a group of young people, all of whom were physically challenged in one way or another. One young woman traced the profile—the eye sockets, the lips, the nose, the ears—of the young person next to her with her fingertips. Then, she tipped her head to one side and laughed a tiny little laugh of total delight. "You're beautiful!" she said. "Just beautiful."

The young woman who had traced the face with such loving care was blind. Her head tilted back, you could see that her eyes were vacant, scarred over, tipped up against her forehead. She saw nothing. Or maybe the real truth of the matter is that she had learned to see a great deal more than most of us do. Maybe she could see what few of the rest of us with our fine vision and superficial souls could never see.

The scene makes all of us think: What is there about losing something that makes us all the more aware of it? Maybe it is the instinct for life that rises in us only when we lack it.

Maybe that is one of the greater gifts of growing old. When we can no longer walk as fast as we once did, we come to see all the individual flowers, the cracks in the sidewalk, the children along the way, all the more clearly, all the more consciously than we ever have in the past. It seems as if one of the functions of aging is to give us the capacity to see what we've missed all the years before.

Perhaps one of the most important dimensions of aging is to bring us to understand that life cannot be taken for granted. Life cannot be devoured—it can only be savored. It is to be sipped and drunk to the dregs.

Unfortunately, in a society geared to overdrive, tasting and savoring are not the character of our days. We live in rush-hour traffic, tapping our fingers on the steering wheel. We even pursue our faith lives on schedule. No "little visits" here; no meditation time on the riverbank. No long talks about spiritual problems or philosophical questions with old friends. We're too busy being alive to pause long enough to live well.

But now that is all over. In every loss and limitation I face lies an invitation to go more deeply into life than I have been doing. When breath comes with more difficulty, I smell the air—often for the first time in years. When I see the days running out, each becomes more of an adventure if I will only make it so. When people before me start to disappear from my life in a heartbreakingly regular way, I begin to talk more to those around me about important things, for fear I may not have enough time to teach them what I did not know myself before.

Now I begin to look back, to collect from memory what I overlooked during all the years of running and gathering and garnering and changing and disposing of people and things so casually along the way. And as I collect, I develop enough soul myself to finally appreciate the place of all these others in my life. From one, I got a model of the discipline I needed. From another the love of work that made my life an enterprise in creativity rather than a drudge. From a third, an introduction to life and how to live it with maturity as well as excitement.

Summer heat is more welcome now when I get colder easier. Winter wind and lashing rain become more friend than enemy as I snuggle up with a warm quilt and a good book. Autumn, I come to realize, is more the promise of another, brighter spring than the dull, gray end of life.

The burden of having to confront these lost years lies in the fear that I have missed most of my life while I was living it head up and running.

The blessing lies in the fact that I not only come to appreciate the past, but also the present in a whole new way.

FAITH

"We hope to grow old, yet we fear old age," the French essayist Jean de La Bruyère said. "We are willing to live and afraid to die."

It is difficult to know what we fear more: death or old age? It may well be that we fear both age and death in equal portions, but because we fear death we accept old age—with great reluctance. We really want to be young because we have no idea how wonderful old age can be. We want to live because we do not understand death, the birth canal of what the spirit says must surely be a new, another kind of life. Whatever it might be. But it is the darkness that surrounds that "whatever" that arrests both our thoughts and our feelings.

Darkness is the pathology of the soul. It comes out of the awareness that however competent I am in life—I keep a good home, I raised good children, I have a position of some influence—there will come a time when I find myself facing a moment over which I have absolutely no control. I will die.

What's more, I do not really know what will be required of

me then. I have no idea what the moment will be like. I only know that I will be alone. I will travel this road unaccompanied, go through it by myself, face life's greatest venture without caretakers, without companions, without support. There will be no one who can go with me down this tunnel into nowhere. It is the moment of absolute surrender.

But not until. Not until I have sucked every minute out of life I can. Not until I have fought for every breath I have. Not until I have more faith in the spiritual meaning of this time of life than I do at the present moment. Not until I see that the God who created me, who grew me to full stature, is not finished with my growing yet.

It's not so much a final judgment that we fear. We have failed often, yes, but, most of us, most of the time, have done everything we could do under the stress of the moment at hand. Our failures have been legion, yes, but our malice has been minimal. True, we have never been quite as uncontaminated of soul as we would have liked to be, but our efforts have been real. So, whatever our questions about God, about Life, about the End, we have a certain confidence in our lack of confidence in the unknown. We are not sure who God is, of course, but we are confidently sure of who or what God is not.

We believed in the ideals. We often found them difficult to choose between—when one was in tension with another—but we believed in both charity and justice, for instance. We believed in both law and mercy, even when we leaned more toward one than the other. Even if our struggles to do more, to be better, have not been as mighty as they could have been, we never gave up trying to live within the boundaries of the best. Even if we never really had the character to be absolute in all dimensions, we believed.

Until now. Until the days began to shorten. Until we woke up one day and knew without a doubt that we had far more time behind us than before us.

The problem is that we are not sure if we have faith in faith. We are putting it to the test the only way we know. We are doubting whether we have it at all. We wonder if we have enough. We wonder what happened to the faith we did have. Once. When we were young. And was that kind of faith really faith at all? Or was it magic? And does that niggling little desire for clarity over questions nullify whatever faith we do have?

The irony of the struggle is that this unknowing is, in the end, what faith is about.

Surely one of the purposes of life is to bring us to the point where we come to trust the universe, to recognize the logic of its apparent chaos in our lives—snowstorms in winter, blazing heat in the summertime, death in autumn. But that kind of great, openhearted trust comes slowly. It comes only to those who can look back down the years and realize that tragedies turned into blessings. In the end.

Only as the years went by did we painstakingly, tardily, begin to understand that there is blessing in the cosmos. Before technology, God was.

We cooked food with fire then. Not simply in Neanderthal times but in our own, as well. We cured meat with salt. We ground wheat with wind and water. We came to realize that, both as a human race and as a people, we had been given everything we needed to live and we could get it by ourselves. Food came fresh, not vacuum packed. Water came from the stream, not the tap. Light came every day and we slept through darkness. Between us and the elements was the miracle called Life and the God who made them regular as dawn, constant as the mountains. We came to realize that there is an essential goodness all around us, holding us up, carrying us on.

But we are beginning to realize that we have only partially come to see. Now all those realizations flow over into our soul and soften our fears of the darkness whose end we do not know.

We have practiced faith all our lives, of course. But in such transitory things. We trusted banks that failed and governments that lied to us. We put our faith in credentials that faded and positions that disappeared and money that failed to satisfy. We put our trust in ourselves and called it faith. Now we are learning, as our own life force begins to fade, that we must take our faith and put it elsewhere.

Now we are in the years where we must begin to let go, like a child being lowered into seawater. Having things, being in charge, is not so important anymore. Or as the sixth-century Syrian philosopher Philoxenos wrote: "It is not they who have many possessions who are rich but they who have no needs."

A burden of these years is that we are tempted to think that once we ourselves are no longer powerful enough to work our will on the world around us, we are at the mercy of a cruel universe.

A blessing of these years is that we are now beginning to trust in the life-giving God we do not see, more than we have trusted in the accessories of life which we have seen both come without guarantee and go without warning.

LEGACY

"Nothing is more dishonorable than the old, heavy with years," Seneca wrote, "who have no other evidence of having lived long except age."

Something almost unbearably painful revolves around the graves of unknown soldiers, around potters' fields, around unclaimed bodies in city morgues. But it is not only the anonymity of death that weighs so heavily here. It is surely because a life is gone from us and we have no way of knowing what legacy it left behind.

But there is a big difference between leaving a legacy and leaving a "legacy."

In modern society, to leave a "legacy" ordinarily means to specify the distribution of property—money, in most cases—to heirs according to the terms described in the legal document known as a will. It's a relatively rare event for most people to be mentioned in a will.

And yet, people talk all the time about how the life of the person, now deceased, has enriched them. The common denominator of all deaths—rich or poor, male or female, powerful or powerless—is not the will, not the money. It is the immaterial legacy, the true enrichment, each of us has gained by having our lives touched by those who have gone before us.

And those legacies are not rare at all. They are what connects us both to the past and to the future.

What we are inclined to forget is that each of us leaves a legacy, whether we mean to, whether we want to or not. Our legacies are the quality of the lives we leave behind. What we have been will be stamped on the hearts of those who survive us for years to come. The only question is, will we cultivate that living legacy as carefully as bankers and tax collectors and lawyers do the material wills that distribute nothing but stocks and bonds and insurance policies and savings accounts which might disappear with the legal fees they generate?

What are we leaving behind? That is the question that marks the timbre of a lifetime.

We leave behind our attitude toward the world. We are re-membered for whether or not we inspired in others a love for life and an openness to all of those who lived it with us. We will be remembered for our smiles and for our frowns, for our laughter and for our complaints, for our kindness and for our selfishness.

We leave behind for all the world to see the value system that marks everything we do. People who never asked us directly what we valued in life never doubt for a moment what it was. They know if we cared for the Earth because they watched us as we seeded our flowerbeds—or let the debris from the garage spill over into what could have been a garden. They know what we thought of people of other colors or creeds by the language we used and the lives we connected with. They know the depth of our spiritual life by the way we treated those around us and what we thought of life and what we gave our lives to doing.

We leave behind the memory of the way we treated strangers, how we loved the individuals closest to us, how we cared for those who loved us, how we spoke to them in hard times, how we gave ourselves away to satisfy their needs.

We leave behind, in our very positions on death and life, on purpose and meaning, a model of relationship with God. Our own spiritual life is both challenge and support to the spiritual struggles of those around us. As they themselves approach the moment of truth, like us, they look for models of what it means to go beyond speculation, despite uncertainty.

Our legacy is far more than our fiscal worth. Our legacy does not end the day we die. We have added to it every moment of our lives. It is the crowning moment of the aging process. It is the major task of these years. In this period of life, we have both the vision and the wisdom to see that the legacy is what we want it to be.

If we need to erase old memories and create new ones, this is the time to do it.

If we have lived an unbalanced life, more emphasis on consumption and accumulation than on giving and sharing and saving, these are the years in which to change our way of living so that others can live well.

If we have neglected the development of the spirit for the sake of the material, we have the time now to think again about what it means to be alive, to be full of life, to love all of life, to be full of God. These can be the years when our spirits soar beyond any old injuries, above all the old pettiness, overcome all the engrained prejudices that have kept us from enriching our lives with friends who are black and brown and yellow and red and white. Who are other than we are. Whose lives are different than ours. Who have much to teach us about the many other ways of being in this world.

If we need to rethink all the old ideas that are now so much in conflict with the world around us, if we need to rethink even our notion of God, now is the time to give ourselves to the real issues of life. The issues that are not jobs and money, prestige and status, superiority and arrogance.

It is time to ask ourselves what legacy we are leaving behind. Because one thing is sure: whether or not we give much thought to it, everyone else we know will.

A burden of these years is to give in to the thought that personal spiritual growth is no longer an issue for us and so leave the world a legacy of incompleteness.

A blessing of these years is to have the time to complete in ourselves what has been neglected all these years, so that the legacy we leave to others is equal to the full potential within us.

AFTERWORD

The Twilight Time

Grow old along with me!
The best is yet to be,
The last of life, for which the first was made:
Our times are in His hand
Who saith "A whole I planned,
Youth shows but half;
Trust God: see all, nor be afraid!"

ROBERT BROWNING

Sean walks a couple miles every day and continues to write and research. Bill tees off at 6 a.m. every morning and handles his real estate work the rest of the day. Dick and his wife, Willie, take a trip to somewhere new in the world every year and do community service work in between. Treva still does bedside nursing every single day. Annie and Sophie never miss a card game. Mary Margaret does spiritual direction at the prison. Bernie is a hospital chaplain who walks miles of corridors visiting sick people, consoling families she will never see again. Maureen, a financial manager, goes to the office to deal with hundreds of thousands of dollars of income from one fiscal year to another.

They're an impressive group. They make the world go round. They are the center of their families, the voice of their era, the memory of their groups. The real beauty of them, however, is that none of them are unusual. Their numbers are legion.

Millions of other people just like them are doing the same kinds of things every day. And, like them, they are all between the ages of seventy and ninety.

They are healthy and happy, alert and active, full of life and very, very productive. But don't be fooled; they—and all of us—will all slow down before it's over.

Then will come the twilight time, that space between here and there, between earth and eternity, when we begin to be more there than here. When the concerns of this world fade away and we begin to be concentrated somewhere else.

That does not mean that this last period of life is an inactive time, a meaningless time. Not at all.

This may be the time in the nursing home, in the hospital, in the housing complex infirmary when, focused like laser beams, we see life—our own and everybody else's—with fresh and un-canny awareness. We begin to understand things we never even contemplated before, like the meaning of time, the preemi-nence of beauty, the power of the touch of a hand.

Then, little by little, the old cares begin to dim. Nothing seems so important today as it did yesterday. All those things, too, we know—all those things which once consumed us with their demands—will fail to grip us anymore. They will also one day disappear into the cauldron of life and be melted down into nothingness.

We gave our lives to such things once and now can hardly remember what they were anymore. We cried over them and fretted over them, we ended relationships because of them and began other relationships for the very same reason. We gave our lives to what we know now were very little things. We are, now, at peace.

The raging has ended. The dying has begun. Life has done its best with us. We are finished now, except for the finishing. We have bigger things to think about now than the things that, up to now, have consumed us. Instead, we must figure out now how to say goodbye to those who refuse to admit that we're going. We must determine how to live in this new, quiet way. We must stir up enough energy in us to be present, one last time at least, to those who come to be present to us.

But our own work is not yet complete.

The twilight time, like all the time before it, is not for nothing. It has its own tasks, its burdens, its subtle gifts to give us.

The twilight time is time for trust. It's all out of our hands now. We have used our last years well. We have lived with all the energy we had. And now we must trust the time of no energy at all to make us open in a different way to those around us. We must trust our doctors and our caregivers and our situation and our passage. We must allow ourselves to be cared for and trust that the people doing it are receiving something from us, as we receive from them.

We must summon the patience that pain takes or that breathing demands or that the schedules of others impose on us. We must give ourselves to the process of dying one muscle, one moment at a time.

There is time now for a new kind of strength, as well as for the weakness that culls it. It takes strength to bear well what we cannot do a thing to change.

There is a strength, a new kind of dignity, that comes with bearing weakness well, for smiling when there is nothing much to smile about by pedestrian standards, for believing that death is the birthing passage to a new life.

It's time now for surrender to acceptance. Perhaps for the first time in our adult lives we will go into a period of total dependence. We will be asked to accept rather than to resist, to welcome instead of to question, to believe instead of to doubt.

There will be conversations yet to have. This is our last time to be honest, to be loving, to be open, to be grateful, to be patient, to be lovable and loving and loved.

This is the time for melting into God. The words that come now will be the honest ones, the hopeful ones. This time will be the culmination of all the learning of all the other years. The veil between us and eternity will begin to tear and we will begin the slow walk through it, ready, open, thrown upon the heart of God.

We know now that this life is whole. The first part was good, so good. Why would we doubt for a moment that this half will be anything less?

Now the Mystery is about to reveal itself. Now the time is complete. Now it is finished. Now it is only beginning.

Endnotes

1. McKinsey and Co., New York City, www.harpers.org/HarpersIndex2006-10.html (accessed January 23, 2007).
2. Nancy R. Hooyman and H. Asuman Kiyak, *Social Gerontology: A Multidisciplinary Perspective*, 6th ed. (Boston: Allyn and Bacon, 2002), 28.
3. The 2005 National Health Interview Survey, www.cdc.gov/nchdata/nhis/earlyrelease/200509_12.pdf
4. James Hillman, *The Force of Character: And the Lasting Life* (New York: Random House/Ballantine Books, 1999), 17.
5. Patricia Beattie Jung, "Differences Among the Elderly: Who is on the Road to Breman?" in Stanley Hauerwas, Carole Bailey Stoneking, Keith G. Meador, and David Cloutier, eds., *Growing Old in Christ* (Grand Rapids, MI: Wm. B. Eerdmans, 2003), 112-113.
6. Soldo and Manton, in E. B. Palmore, *Ageism: Negative and Positive*, 1990, in "Ageism," University of California, Berkeley, www.socrates.berkeley.edu/~aging/ModuleAgeism.html (accessed February 11, 2007).
7. Palmore, Crimmins, Saito, and Ingegneri, in E. B. Palmore, *Ageism: Negative and Positive*, 1990, in "Ageism," University of California, Berkeley, www.socrates.berkeley.edu/~aging/ModuleAgeism.html (accessed February 11, 2007).
8. Palmore, in E. B. Palmore, *Ageism: Negative and Positive*, 1990, in "Ageism," University of California, Berkeley, www.socrates.berkeley.edu/~aging/ModuleAgeism.html (accessed February 11, 2007).
9. Poon, in E. B. Palmore, *Ageism: Negative and Positive*, 1990, in "Ageism," University of California, Berkeley, www.socrates.berkeley.edu/~aging/ModuleAgeism.html (accessed February 11, 2007).
10. Gail Sheehy, *New Passages: Mapping Your Life Across Time* (New York: Random House/Ballantine Books, 1995), 373.
11. Hooyman and Kiyak, 19.
12. www.archomaha.com/Pastoral/FamilyLifeOffice/AgingMinistries/agingministries.html (accessed February 2, 2007).
13. Hooyman and Kiyak, 19.
14. U.S. Department of Labor – Women's Bureau, January 2005.
15. George E. Vaillant, M.D., *Aging Well* (New York: Little, Brown, 2002), 334-336.
16. Daniel Okrent, "Twilight of the Boomers," *Time*, June 12, 2000.
17. Vaillant, 213.
18. Hooyman and Kiyak, 153.
19. Vaillant, 246.
20. Gallup Poll 2006, www.pollingreport.com (accessed January 23, 2007).
21. Associated Press Poll 2005, www.usatoday.com (accessed January 26, 2007).
22. Bill Wallace, "McNamara Comes Clean About the Vietnam War," *San Francisco Chronicle*, www.sfgate.com (accessed February 12, 2007).
23. Population Profile of the United States: 2000 U.S. Census Bureau.
24. Vaillant, 215-216.

Acknowledgments

I am grateful to the people whose works are cited in this book both for the precision of their research on aging as well as for their commitment to this important subject. Because of them and those like them, this society will be able to profit from the experience, creativity, and wisdom of older people as they never have before.

I am always and forever grateful to those whose ongoing support of this work brings continuing organization and quality to the structure, process, and state of the manuscript. Those include: Susan Doubet, OSB who prepares the manuscript and traces and confirms every item in the work; Marlene Bertke, OSB whose copy reading is flawless; and Maureen Tobin, OSB whose long-term assistance coordinates every facet of the writing process and makes it all possible.

Most especially, I am grateful to the readers whose own life experience has given direction and depth to this work. These people from various walks of life compared the ideas here to their own circumstances and background and gave significant direction to the final shaping of the content. These editorial readers include Helen Boyle, the Rev. Dr. Fred Burnham, the Rev. Dr. Joan Brown Campbell, Mary Delaney, Dr. Jack Delaney, Dr. Gail Grossman Freyne, Russ and Kathy Peace, Dr. Sara Pitzer, Sue Pucker, Teresa Wilson and the women of Pilgrim Place, as well as my own Benedictine sisters Carolyn Gorny-Kopkowski, OSB, Mary Lou Kownacki, OSB, Rosanne Loneck, OSB, Anne McCarthy, OSB, Mary Miller, OSB, and Ellen Porter, OSB.

Finally, I am especially grateful to Denise Robison, past Deputy Secretary of the Pennsylvania Department of Aging and current member of the Pennsylvania Council on Aging. Denise's professional background, knowledge, and current involvement in the field brought an important level of expertise and confirmation to the accuracy of the data as well as to the ideas included in the manuscript.

In whatever way I have failed to respond to all these suggestions and insights, I alone am responsible for whatever weakness in the text that may imply.

Most of all, I am grateful to those older people in my life who have brought me to recognize and value the role of the wisdom generation in all our lives.